BEYOND
the Scars

daring to live forward

F. ELAINE OLSEN

BEYOND the Scars

daring to live forward

NyreePress

F. ELAINE OLSEN

© 2012, 2014 by F. Elaine Olsen. All rights reserved.

Cover Photo: Istock Photo.
Cover design by Tekeme Studios.

Published by NyreePress Literary Group (www.nyreepress.com). NyreePress functions only as book publisher. As such, the ultimate design, content, editorial accuracy, and views expressed or implied in this work are those of the author.

No part of this publication may be reproduced, stored in a retrieval system, or transmitted in any way by any means—electronic, mechanical, photocopy, recording, or otherwise—without the prior permission of the copyright holder, except as provided by USA copyright law.

Unless otherwise noted, all scriptures are taken from the *Holy Bible, New International Version®, NIV®*. Copyright © 1973, 1978, 1984 by Biblica, Inc.™ Used by permission of Zondervan. All rights reserved worldwide. www.zondervan.com

Print   ISBN 978-0-9915412-2-5
Ebook ISBN 978-0-9915412-3-2
Library of Congress Catalog Card Number: 2014935286

Dedication

Courageous is the soul who contends with suffering, wrestles with suffering, lays claim to a stronger spirit because of suffering, and refuses to retreat from the battle until something is gained from the suffering. Even if that something is as small (or as huge) as befriending another soul walking a similar path.

Judith Guerino was that friend for me. This book is lovingly dedicated to her life and witness. Her courage lives on inside of me.

Contents

Acknowledgments ix
Prologue xi

1. Poverty Is a Good Starting Point 1
2. Cancer Gives Back 5
3. Unwrapping the Unexpected 9
4. Everybody Has Something 13
5. Everybody Has a Story 17
6. Taking Good Care of Your Heart 21
7. Living Up to Your Learning 25
8. Real Love Looks Beyond the Scars 29
9. God Keeps Pace with Your Pain 33
10. Suffering Need Needs a Suffering Friend 37
11. Making an Apology to Suffering 41
12. Living Up to Your Convictions 45
13. Just Breathe 49
14. Wearing Your Remembrance 53
15. God Knows Who You Are 57
16. Montana Is Real 61
17. There Is a Certain Place 65
18. Ascending to Your Overlook 69
19. Living Your Greater Thing 73

20. Grieving Your Losses 77
21. Affording Them Grace 81
22. Hope Grows 85
23. Holding On to Your Faith 89
24. Speaking Your Faith 93
25. Turning the Page 97
26. Embracing Quietness 103
27. Surviving Is a Collective Effort 107
28. Gracing the Stage You Stand Upon 111
29. Clutching Truth 115
30. Never Take More Than You Need 119
31. Sending Flowers to the Living 123
32. Rethinking Time 127
33. Pressing On 131
34. Seasons Change 135
35. Live On 139
36. Be Prepared to Give an Answer 143
37. Eden Is Closer Now Than It Has Ever Been 149
38. God Will Take You Across the River 153
39. God Is Next 157
40. God Is Faithful 161
Epilogue 167
Postscript 170
Endnotes 172

Acknowledgments

THIS BOOK IS a collaborative effort, representing the many participants who've linked arms with me in my fight for survivorship. I've been blessed with an abundance of friends, family members, and people in the medical community who have willingly and sacrificially supported me throughout this season. I consider them survivors alongside of me. And while it's not possible for me to acknowledge each of them with the thanks they deserve, I want to take a moment to extend my gratitude to a few people who have been directly connected to my work on this book.

Billy, I love being your bride. Never have our vows rung truer than in this last year of our marriage. Other than God, you were the only person who knew I was writing this book. Your daily encouragement during those hot, crowded days of summer gave me the strength I needed to see this project through to the finish. You are my Ephesians 5:25.

Mom, I love being your daughter. You've mothered me well. Your presence in and out of our home during my treatment phase brought certain stability to the ground beneath our feet. You are full of courage and comfort, both of which you've extended to me in large measure. At a time in your life when you might have thought your best mothering days were behind you, your heart rallied around mine and drew me close to your spirit. This has been your finest hour, and I am indebted to and humbled by your generous love for me. I am also exceedingly grateful for your editing eye.

Nick, Colton, Jadon, and Amelia, I love being your mom. Your contribution to this book has been the unconditional affection you've showered upon me in my time of need. You gave me a reason to fight when all I wanted to do was quit. My prayer for each one of you is that one day you might read these words and draw strength from them for your own seasons of struggle. You are my legacy, my letter to the world, my four beautiful graces from God. I hold you close in my heart.

My medical team (Dr. Habal, Dr. Bakri, Dr. Patel, Colleen, Patsy, and Sarah), I love being your patient. Thank you for always treating me like a person instead of a paycheck. Your careful watch over me has played a vital role in my survivorship and has given me an opportunity to write this book to serve as an encouragement for other patients on a similar journey.

Sheri Kaetzel and her team of contributors, I love being your friend. Thanks to your collective generosity, I was able to attend a recent writer's conference. Your push to get me there served as a catalyst to writing this book. Had I not felt the pressure of a deadline, these words wouldn't have come about as quickly and as certainly as they did. God's hands were all over this. I just couldn't see them at the time.

My online community of believers, I love the faith that we share. Even though many of us have never met face-to-face, our connection is strong because of Jesus Christ. Thank you for the genuine support you've given to me throughout my cancer season and beyond. You add value to my life through your prayers, your presence, and your support of my writing endeavors.

Sister and brother survivors, I love your courageous spirits. To those who've gone before me, to those I've met along the way, to those who currently stand beside me, and to those who will share in my journey through the reading of this book, you are the reasons behind my words. I pray you find a measure of comfort and companionship here.

Prologue
Daring to Live Forward

See, I am doing a new thing! Now it springs up; do you not perceive it? I am making a way in the desert and streams in the wasteland.
—Isaiah 43:19

GROWING UP, I wasn't one to take a dare. The dare was often attached to the wrong side of what I knew to be right, and the fear of potential consequences (should I get caught) was enough to keep me firmly rooted on the right side of what I knew to be right. But every now and again, other dares would surface in my life—ones that challenged me to take a risk on the right side of right, to manifest personal courage in order to explore and dream beyond the safety of known and comfortable borders. Those were the kinds of dares I was more inclined to accept, because somewhere deep within, I understood that in refusing to take those dares, I would be missing out on life as it was meant to be lived—a life lived forward instead of a life stuck "on hold."

A dare to give a speech.
A dare to write a composition for critique.
A dare to sing a solo.
A dare to go to college.
A dare to love.
A dare to marry.
A dare to leave home.
A dare to have children.

Beyond the Scars: Daring to Live Forward

A dare to preach and lead.
A dare to dream.
A dare to revise that dream.
A dare to trust doctors.
A dare to wait.
A dare to hope.
A dare to trust God.

In the acceptance of these dares, I am learning what it means to live forward—to grow and become more of the woman that God created me to be. My choices for courageous living haven't always yielded the results I imagined on the front side of my acceptance. But even then, especially then, those choices have moved me toward a more purposeful life. Living forward is always a choice, one in which our will is the deciding factor. We can opt for a life on hold or a life lived forward, no matter the circumstances.

Not long ago, life presented me with a dare to live . . . *beyond my scars*. There was no doubt regarding the scarring that would take place in my flesh; my life depended on it. There was, however, a reasonable doubt as to how I would respond to those scars. Would they define my witness or would I courageously step beyond the wounding and allow them to refine it?

I chose to look the dare squarely in the eye and boldly proclaim my acceptance of this challenge to live beyond my scars. Why? Because I wanted to do more than just survive the wounds that had left those scars on my flesh and in my spirit. I didn't want to simply co-exist with my scars for my remaining days; I wanted to live more fully because of them. To give them their due, to courageously allow them their work within me, and then to take the best of that difficult shaping and offer it as an encouragement to others who are walking in similar stride.

Maybe you are that person, someone wounded and bloodied by a recent suffering. The scars run deep, and you are struggling to live forward. Courage has left the building, and you want to hide within the safety of what's known and comfortable rather than venture outside to see if there might possibly be life beyond your scars. The misguided allegiance you feel toward your scars is stronger than your allegiance to live more fully because of them. Accordingly, you're stuck, stalled in between "what has been" and "what could be."

I understand. I know what it is be stuck in my scars. I also know what it is to live beyond them. Mind you, not without them; scars remain as a tangible witness to the suffering season I have known. But these days, my scars are no longer a hindrance to my forward progression. Instead, they fuel it, pushing me onward toward wholeness and

Prologue

daring me to give them over to God so that he might, in turn, make them count for more than simply the pain I've endured.

This is my sole hope for the words written here, that they would serve as an invitation to you to step forward in your journey beyond the scars that remain as a painful witness in your life. Your suffering may not be the same as mine. My nemesis is named *cancer*. Perhaps your adversary is more easily identified by words like divorce, unemployment, addiction, infertility, bankruptcy, loneliness, death of a loved one, loss of a dream, and the like. Regardless of the suffering that has scarred your history, you have the final word regarding your wounds. You, alone, get to choose what you will make of them.

My prayer is that you will allow God to make them count for all eternity. With every word that you read here and with every word that you write and speak in response to what you've read here, may those words serve as your personal declaration over your pain. The eyes of the Lord are on us, and his deliverance is certain for those of us who tether our expectations to the loving work of the cross. Place your hope in Jesus, and if you're willing, place your hand in mine. Together, let's walk forward beyond our scars.

Go ahead. I dare you.

Elaine

Poverty Is a Good Starting Point

"I tell you the truth," he said, "this poor widow has put in more than all the others. All these people gave their gifts out of their wealth; but she out of her poverty put in all she had to live on."

—Luke 21:3–4

OUT OF MY poverty . . .

This is where I begin, where I lay down my pen as an offering before the Lord. It would be easier to walk away from my story, to keep my words to myself—words buried deep within, words not yet realized, words trapped beneath the weightiness of my recent cancer season. With the dig will come discovery, of this I am certain. The revelation may not be what you're looking for, and because of this, my heart grows weary and faint with the wondering.

Will they be enough, Lord? Are these words worth fighting for? Is there ample ink left in my well—enough words and enough willingness—to write this chapter of my story? Will this surrender be costly? Will the end result reflect the fight required to get there? Will joy replace current sorrow? Will fullness replace this emptiness I'm holding? Will hope supplant doubt? Will kingdom work be done through weakness?

Indeed, out of my poverty, I come to the altar of God's grace. Like the widow in Luke 21, there's not much left in my personal coffers, or so it seems. Two small coppers are what remain after a long season of costly suffering. Cancer has brought me to the end of a treacherous, winding road, only to realize that another one awaits me—the road of survival. Two coppers won't get me very far, but my releasing them to God? Well, perhaps they'll carry me further than what my understanding will allow me in this moment.

Beyond the Scars: Daring to Live Forward

    I love the widow's giving story, penned some two thousand years prior to mine. Hers moved the heart of Jesus, because out of her poverty, she willingly gave all that she had. I want to give the same . . . to go "all in" with Jesus, believing that on the other side of my costly release, some holy truth will be spoken by the Father on my behalf—words that will serve as a living memorial for the generations to come, who will enter into my story even as I have entered into this widow's.

    I don't imagine the widow had much life left in her when she entered the temple that day. Grief was undoubtedly part of her story, poverty her present reality. Yet her days were underscored by an overriding commitment to her faith, her church, and her God. She gave all that she could; some would say even more than she should. But Jesus would call it enough, "more than all the others." She may not have heard him, may not have been privy to his pleasure in that instance, but I am certain she felt it. Costly surrenders willingly given to God may not feel pleasant prior to their release, but when offered as a final gesture of faith, there's a goodness that gives witness to the moment.

    We don't know what happened to the widow going forward from that one moment. Perhaps that's the point—not what God did for her that day, but rather what she did for God. And while we're only given access to this one window-frame look into her story, something tells me it's one of her most important stories, a life-lesson kind—a teaching memory captured via the lens of God's Word, providing us with a hook to hang our hopes on, fertile soil to live our lives upon, and a firm foundation to heal our hurts within. It is a truth that simply and profoundly validates the impoverished witness of a widow who surrendered "all that she had to live on" into the treasury of God's ministry.

    Yes, this is where I willingly choose to begin this chapter of my story. I don't have much in the way of worldly possessions to surrender into the treasury of God's ministry, but I have this pen in my hand and, every now and again, a few moments of quiet that belong to just Jesus and me. Out of my poverty, I give them both to the Lord, believing him for strength enough to chronicle the witness of my cancer season.

    Poverty is a good starting point for the rich increase of God's immeasurable favor. When we begin there, when we reach the end of ourselves—when the heart beats wearily, the tears come easily, and the coppers are down to two—then we, like the widow, have a hard decision to make: give to God out of our poverty, or give in to it. While both decisions begin with insufficient funds, the former is the only one that will end in surplus, the only one that will seed and grow and multiply with the loving excess of heaven's grace.

    Giving to God out of our poverty is perhaps the greatest act of faith that will ever be credited to our kingdom accounts. Hard surrenders made in the leanest of all of life's seasons indicate an underlying, undeniable, and underscored personal trust in the work of the cross—a bleeding juncture that pinned Christ's sacred flesh to solid faith. Out of

Poverty is a Good Starting Point

his poverty, Jesus deposited his final coppers into the treasury of his Father's ministry. And when Jesus did so, heaven began its accumulation—an exponential increase that continues through us because of the hard surrenders we're willing to deposit into the treasury of God's ministry.

This is my lean season, perhaps the leanest I have ever lived. It is a time of low reserves and few leftovers. In faith, albeit a painfully small measure, I've scraped up my remaining coppers, and I willingly bring them to the altar of God. It's all I have to live on, just a little bit of hope, a little bit of strength, a little bit of a seemingly very little. But something tells me that my impoverished estate just might be the most important "little" of my life.

Perhaps you understand. Perhaps this day you are counting your coppers and coming up short. Your poverty of pocket has cast worry and fear into your heart. Sickness, financial strain, relational hardships, addictions, emotional trauma, and all manner of ills and aches have worked their way into your season, and your faith is delicately dangling on the edge of doubt . . . maybe even a step or two in doubt's direction. You want to quit, want to walk away from your life, want to hang up your hopes and selfishly hold on to the few coins that remain. Surrendering all that you have to live on seems too costly and too little to make much of a difference to anyone.

Like me, and like the widow from two thousand years ago, you have a decision to make. Out of your poverty, you can give all that you have to God, or you can give in to your depletion. Only one choice will lead you to the surplus of heaven. Only one choice will afford you the privilege of seeing the multiplication of God's increase through you. Only one choice will invest your little and grow it into "more than all the others."

Trusting God is that one and only choice, and today, I'm making the decision to do my banking with the King. I cast my two coppers into the treasury and begin with a few words about a fledgling faith and the suffering season that has recently served as the backdrop of my life. And while it seems too little of a thing, it also seems like a good place to start. For whenever a heart is depleted and emptied out, there's room enough for a fresh planting of God.

I certainly could use one. Could you use one as well? Then I invite you to God's temple this day and offer this prayer of initial supplication for a fresh planting from his heart:

With hands wide open, pockets emptied out, and our hearts' strong willingness to trust you with our futures, Father, we come to your treasury this day. Out of our poverty, we offer up to you all that remains in our possession—our gifts, our talents, our time, our energy, our depletion, our failures, our sufferings, and our wills. It seems too small a surrender, Lord; two coppers hardly seem enough. Take them; multiply them; do what you will with them. From our poverty, seed your kingdom. Amen.

Living Forward

- How do you identify with the widow's sacrifice? Are you down to your last coppers? Describe.

- Why might poverty be a good starting point for seeing the rich increase of God's favor? Why might wealth be a detriment?

- When has your costly surrender been replaced by a fresh planting of the Lord?

- Take time to read the widow's story in Luke 21:1–4. What do you see in it? What is God asking you to surrender in this current season of living?

2

Cancer Gives Back

Let us hold unswervingly to the hope we profess, for he who promised is faithful.
—Hebrews 10:23

SHE WAS NEW to our group that night. Several of us had gathered for our monthly meeting at the hospital, all of us with one thing in common—cancer. I was fairly new to the group as well, only finishing my last round of chemotherapy a couple of weeks earlier. Even though I was feeling poorly, I could tell that she felt worse. She introduced herself by telling us about her previous day's diagnosis—breast cancer. Her body language couldn't mask her fear; her voice quivered with apprehension. She was a mess, and I'm afraid that much of the conversation that evening didn't go very far to alleviate her anxieties.

War story after war story commenced, tons of free advice and information as well. Her pen trembled in her hand as she tried to write it all down, take it all in. It was too much too soon, and her fear was palpable. Sensing the need to rein in the conversation, I simply reached over, took her hand, and looked her straight in the eyes while speaking these words: "I know this is a lot. I know this seems bad, and there will be days when it will be bad. But this I also know: You can do this thing. By God's grace and with his help, you can do this. And there will be goodness that comes to you because of this road that you're on."

The room grew silent; her eyes filled with tears, and for the next few moments, she was able to push past her fear in order to take hold of a little hope. Just a little. Just enough to see her through until morning. And with that exchange between us, hope arrived in my heart as well—a gift to me after a long season of struggle and an unwrapping of grace that gently whispered validation into my cancer, meaning into my seemingly meaningless suffering, and purpose into the pain I had endured. Hope came back around and interjected its witness into me so that I would have something more to offer to a hurting heart than casually spoken words of comfort. I could speak hope, because I had hope. Cancer, oddly enough, had afforded me this gift.

Cancer gives back. I know—a provocative thought. It's offensive to some, bittersweet truth to others. I have lived both emotions in the past year. I remember the first time the phrase surfaced in my thoughts during a September afternoon walk. Those were the early days in my cancer journey. Days before its cruelty really took hold of my flesh.

I heartily confess my naiveté when first taking the thought on—my bold determination to search for all the ways that cancer wanted to give back to me, to grow me, to mature me, to mold me into a better version of me. Naiveté aside, I asked one thing of God that afternoon. I asked him for moments of deeper perspective, for times of looking beyond my pain in order to take hold of eternal goodness. If I could do that, then maybe I could turn the tables on cancer's fearful grip. Instead of cursing my cancer, maybe I could find a way to bless it, to raise a toast to hope and say to the world, "The disease that has sought to claim me has instead become the means that God has used to rename me Hope-filled Survivor."

It's taken me the better part of a year to arrive at this place of hope. Cancer has taken me through its paces and afforded me a rigorous workout in regards to personal, emotional, and spiritual pain. But along the way, God has answered my prayer. He's kept my heart willing to unearth multiple goodnesses in the midst of trial.

I've found joy in the middle of tears, faith in the clouds of doubt, hope in the face of fear.

Hope. Who among us couldn't use some hope? Some faith-filled expectation or joyful anticipation? A solid hook of promise to hang our hearts upon? Without hope, we are a heartsick people. Without hope, we stay stuck in our pain, wandering around with confusion and with King Solomon's "Meaningless, meaningless! Everything is meaningless" as our mantra (see Eccles. 1:2). Everything is *not* meaningless. All of life is rife with purpose—suffering seasons included. God is not absent from our pain, and his goodness lies waiting beneath the heaviness of suffering. Sometimes our trials serve as the rich soil for an unearthing of the holiest, most sacred kind of gift, an unexpected gift that arrives on the doorsteps of our hearts for us to unwrap as certain hope.

So I write it again—this most offensive, bittersweet, and hopeful statement that I now hold as personal truth: cancer gives back. It has given more to me than it has taken from me. My prayer is that it will give back to you as well and that in the midst of your

Cancer Gives Back

suffering trial, you will be willing to cast meaningless dialogue aside and dig deeply for sacred truth. Hear my heart when I tell you the same thing that I told my new friend on that evening not long ago: "I know this is a lot. I know this seems bad, and there will be days when it will be bad. But this I also know: You can do this thing. By God's grace and with his help, you can do this. And there will be goodness that comes to you because of this road that you're on."

In the pages that follow, I've reflected upon the hope that has arrived in my heart during my pink-ribboned walk. Many of my reflections have become life lessons for the road ahead. I give them to you, believing that they might serve as your gentle companion for the suffering road that you're traveling.

In time, you'll find a rhythm to your painful season. It takes a while to get over the initial shock of its arrival and to find your pulse again. But as you go and along the way, pay attention to hope. Dig for it as if your life depended on it. Don't give up just because the earth beneath your feet is hardened by doubts and dread. Don't allow your tears to express only your desperation; instead, let them be the water that softens your soil so the spade can go deeper.

The tables can be turned on your suffering. Fears can be replaced with hope, and you can stand alongside me as a survivor and shout, "Meaningful, meaningful; all of life is meaningful!" Thus, I pray:

Grant us courage to dig for goodness, Lord. Grant us strength to hold the shovel, determination to break the soil, endurance to go deeper, and faith enough to believe that when we arrive there, hope will be the gift that emerges. Grow our hope in the days to come. As we unwrap its tattered packaging, let us not be fooled into thinking it is nothing—that our pain and our trials are meaningless and void of purpose. You are the only one who can make sense out of this madness and show us how to turn the tables on our suffering. Come and lead us forward to hope. Amen.

Living Forward

❧ What is your initial reaction to the idea that cancer gives back?

Beyond the Scars: Daring to Live Forward

- What has your suffering season required of you? What are the ways it has given back to you?

- What was the most helpful advice or act of kindness someone extended to you as you began to walk through your trial?

- Read Philippians 1:12–30, and record some of the ways that the apostle Paul's suffering season gave back to him.

3

Unwrapping the Unexpected

Christ in you; the hope of glory.
—Colossians 1:27

THE PACKAGE ARRIVED on time, just a few days before Christmas. It was my gift to myself—a bracelet crafted by a favorite jewelry designer and inscribed with the word *entrusted*. I chose this word as a reminder to myself of the struggle I've been allowed and the story that's being written through me because of it—cancer. I believe the struggle to be a sacred trust that should be invested, not hoarded, not wasted, not kept. Thus, I purchased a dangling token of remembrance to refresh my memory whenever I'm tempted to forget the worthiness attached to this suffering season.

When the UPS delivery truck rounded the corner in my neighborhood, I was ready to receive my package. He didn't need to "knock and drop." Instead, I met him on the front porch, graciously received the familiar box, and headed indoors to begin unwrapping. Why the excitement over a small package? Why all the anticipation over a box arriving from California? One reason—I expected it. I ordered it, wanted it, paid for it, and planned on wearing it. A gift expected is a gift easily received, willingly unwrapped, and joyfully applied to a life anticipating its worthiness.

But what about those other "packages" that arrive on the doorsteps of our lives? The ones we didn't order? Those unexpected deliveries with no return-to-sender option? The boxes that are clearly ours, indicated by the name printed on the tag and underscored for emphasis? What about those packages? What anticipation, expectation, and plans do you have when you receive one of those packages?

Beyond the Scars: Daring to Live Forward

You could ignore it, stick it under a bed, shove it in a corner, or maybe even kick it to the curb. But denying its existence doesn't make it any less relevant in your life. No amount of ignoring, sticking, shoving, and kicking will keep it from being yours. No one else can open it, hold it, examine it, and own it, because you have exclusive rights to your package. It belongs to you. What you choose to do with it, however, is where your preference plays a role.

I received one of those unanticipated deliveries on a hot August afternoon in 2010. The package came crudely wrapped, torn and tattered by the outdoor elements, and carelessly crammed between the screen and the front door of my heart. Loudly, it announced its arrival, rudely interrupting my afternoon peace. I asked those around me if they were expecting a package. I didn't remember ordering it; they didn't either. Rather than kicking it to the curb or hiding it in hopes of forgetting about it, I exercised my preference and began unwrapping it. My mystery was short-lived. As the contents of my package were exposed, I quickly realized there was no denying it, only receiving it in hopes of one day being able to view it as a gift rather than a detriment . . .

Cancer.

How does one unpack that kind of delivery? What's the process for unwrapping and receiving cancer? Greater still, what's the point? Why not shove it aside, pack it away, or bury it in the backyard? Why open up the disease when the only warranty it comes with is certain pain, suffering, and torment? Why give it more attention than it deserves?

These are valid questions, realistic ones. These are questions that perhaps have surfaced for you in the receiving of your personal package, questions I've asked of myself, and certainly inquiries I've made of God. The dialogue is never wasted, because with the asking of difficult questions, we arrive at some firmer conclusions regarding the contents of our boxes. Not all of us will choose the same approach towards disclosure, but all of us will be given a choice. We can either receive our packages willingly or with hardened rejection. Either way, they are ours to manage. No one gets a pass when cancer is wedged between the screen and the front door of a heart.

I marvel still at my reasoned response to cancer's arrival. The peace I felt can only be explained by the grace of God that I've experienced throughout my lifetime. When cancer came knocking, God asked me to keep exercising my confidence and trust in him for the revealed contents of my box. There was more than wounding to be found inside its tattered wrapping. Beneath all the painful requirements of the enclosed disease, if I would dig deeply enough, search long enough, open up my heart enough, then I would discover God's "more than enough": A gift—Christ in me, the ribbon of hope that threads me back home to heaven; God in my box, the hope alongside me as we walk the suffering road together.

Unwrapping the Unexpected

Today I wear the gift of Christ's companionship alongside my bracelet of remembrance. Indeed, I've been *entrusted* with the contents of my box . . . with a story that includes cancer, with the unwrapping of pain, and through that pain, with the unwrapping of holy truth, consecrated understanding, sacred intimacy—hallowed ground where the glory of God is revealed in unimaginable measure for the good of the kingdom and for the gain of heaven.

Before I received my package, I had no idea it was heading to my doorstep. Had I known, I might have changed addresses in advance of its arrival. But knowing what I know now—holding the rich truth of Jesus in my heart because of the disease I've been allowed—I would have been more gracious with receiving it. The contents of my package have exceeded my expectations. Cancer has given back to me more than it has taken from me.

Perhaps this day an unexpected package has arrived in your life, wedged in between the screen and the front door of your heart. It may be wrapped with all kinds of warning labels, perhaps weathered by the winds of adversity that have carried it to your doorstep. It's most likely an unwelcomed package. You didn't order it, and you certainly didn't anticipate it.

You have a hard decision to make: reception or rejection of its contents. Either way, it's not going away. Some packages belong to you and you alone. I would never want to underestimate or minimize the contents of your box. That isn't my job, nor is it my judgment. I simply want to ask if you are willing to open it alongside me and alongside God. There is a holy unearthing awaiting your consent—something so deep and so beyond what currently meets your eyes, an unseen glory not yet realized in your heart. I've seen it in my own life; I'm now sharing that vision with you through this book.

My prayer is that you will take the hand of Jesus and start the unwrapping process so that you can discover more fully the ribbon of hope that threads us all back to God. Jesus Christ is that hope—the greatest expectation that can be found wedged in between the screen door and the front door of our hearts. We journey not alone. Thus, I pray:

Grant us willing courage, Father, to begin the process of discovery. Sit beside us as we unwrap our boxes and begin to dig for holy truth. Let not the suffering camouflage the truth. Instead, let it be the avenue of your unveiling, the means through which we begin to see Christ in us, the hope of glory. Comfort us as we walk through this season, and reassure us of your presence when the box seems empty, null and void of purpose. As we surrender our hearts for the dig, unearth your faithfulness, and bring us hope. Keep us faithful to the struggling road, and keep us watching for the unseen graces you send to us along the way. Amen.

Living Forward

- What unanticipated "package" has recently shown up on the doorstep of your heart? Name it, and describe the warning labels that came on the box.

- Have you begun the unwrapping? If so, what are you discovering about the box's contents? If not, what is keeping you from looking inside?

- The unanticipated arrival of packages is replete in Scripture. Take time to reflect on the following passages to uncover the witness of an ancient people who, like us, had a hard choice to make regarding their responses to their boxes. Record your honest responses to theirs.

    - Job 1:1–22
    - Acts 7:54–60
    - 2 Corinthians 12:1–10

4

Everybody Has Something

"I have told you these things, so that in me you may have peace. In this world you will have trouble. But take heart! I have overcome the world."
—John 16:33

EVERYBODY HAS SOMETHING.

Your "something" might not be my something, but at some point in your life, you've had a something. Maybe not a big something, but something large enough to rock your inner equilibrium and force your outward response. It's not particularly important what your something is. What is important is what you do with your something. Somethings come and go; what will endure, however, is the memory of how you handled yours.

Whatever trips you up is your something. I've been known to say this to others who make mention of their somethings to me. In my recent season, many have been careful not to speak their somethings in my direction for fear they might add to my something. If they do speak, there's almost always an apologetic tone mingled in with their declaration.

"Elaine, my back is giving me fits right now; I can barely get out of bed. But that's nothing compared to what you're going through."

Do you hear the apology? The minimizing of personal need? Her something *is* something, and I imagine it's tripping her up from time to time, if not physically, then certainly emotionally, mentally, or spiritually.

How about these somethings I've heard about in recent days, almost always ringing with a similar apologetic tone:

- My husband is having an affair, but . . .
- I'm depressed; I don't know if I can make it, but . . .
- My sixteen-year-old daughter is pregnant, but . . .
- The people in my church don't like me, but . . .
- My husband has trouble breathing in this heat, but . . .
- I've just lost my home in a tornado, but . . .
- I'm overweight, and I'm embarrassed about it, but . . .
- I'm retired, and I feel so lost right now, but . . .
- My husband and I are close to declaring bankruptcy, but . . .
- I don't know where my eighteen-year-old daughter is living right now, but . . .
- My mother's just been diagnosed with Alzheimer's, but . . .
- My car broke down, but . . .
- I've got the flu, but . . .
- My daughter is autistic, but . . .
- My son's in detention, but . . .
- My husband's leaving for another tour of duty, but . . .
- The money's run out, but . . .
- The love's grown cold, but . . .
- _____ (fill in the blank with your current something), but it's nothing compared to what you're going through!

Before long, these very weighty somethings are reduced to nothing because the owners of said somethings (at least when talking with me) are using the wrong set of lenses to assess the impact of their personal pain. They're using my cancer as the benchmark against which to measure their suffering seasons. Again, my reminder to them and to you, "Whatever trips you up." Whatever the scenario, whether considered big or small from an earthly perspective, if it's tripping you up—if it's eating away at you on the inside—then consider your something the one thing that must be dealt with.

My something is breast cancer. Do you have cancer? Before you answer that question, let me rephrase it and allow you to sit with it for a minute or two.

Do you have a disease where abnormal body cells are multiplying at a rapid rate, replacing and invading the normal, healthy cells in your body? Is there some damaged DNA contained within your cells that is replicating out of control, taking on the form of a tumor or taking flight within your bloodstream?

This definition of cancer comes from the American Cancer Society, and according to their website, half of all men and one-third of all women will develop cancer.[1] These

Everybody Has Something

are staggering statistics; the odds aren't in our favor for a cancer-free existence. If you manage to miss cancer's roll call, there are others who won't—friends, co-workers, spouses, children, extended family members. All of us know someone who has battled this disease. Cancer is not exclusive in its territory. It crosses all barriers to invade the normal soil of our everyday lives and to raise its flag of abnormality.

As common as cancer is, you'd think we'd get used to the announcement of another name added to the roll, but we are almost always shocked by its arrival. Cancer is the six-letter word that wields enough power to immediately strike a death blow into the heart of hope, a word that can bend the knees of the most proud, bow the heart of the worst sinner, and rock the faith of the holiest of saints.

Cancer is indeed something—my something. And while it gets a lot of press and a lot of sympathy and compassion, in this season of suffering, I've been reflecting on those lesser-known "cancers," the ones that attack us from the outside-in rather than the other way around. Those pains, aches, and invasions of all manner of sorrows and problems work their way into our lives and multiply their abnormalities into our hearts and minds. What about those cancers? Might they be just as destructive as mine? Might your something qualify?

I don't want to minimize my something. Breast cancer and everything that comes with such a diagnosis is a formidable foe, not to be taken lightly or casually brushed aside as nothing. It is a big something, and it can easily trip me up at the slightest mention. But I do want to acknowledge that there have been other "cancers" in my forty-five years upon this earth, some of them perhaps even more destructive than the one I'm contending with right now. There were malignancies that took root in my life for a long season, even though the prognosis was promising, and tumors that have stayed because I refused the treatment that would enable their release. I've had a lifetime of somethings that have disabled me, fractured me, mocked me, and maligned me, only to eventually humble me toward healing.

I'm not sure which of my cancers has the upper hand right now—the one that bravely displays the pink ribbon where my breasts used to be or the lesser-known ones that hide beneath the scars of my survivorship. Either way, they're all something, because they all have the capacity to force my stumbling on any given day and to eat away at the health I've previously known.

So let me ask you this question again, even as I am asking the same of myself: Do you have cancer? What's tripping you up? What malignancy is eating away at your heart, mind, and soul? What something is keeping you from being the person God has called you to be? Your something matters to him, whether currently hidden or painfully exposed. You may not wear a pink ribbon like I do, but if your something is prohibiting your good health, then, like me, you must treat your disease with all the care and attention it deserves.

We're part of the something statistic, the something generation. Every name makes the roll call on this one. It's not "half of all men" or "one-third of all women." No one gets a pass. As somethings go, it's 100 percent participation. Make no apologies for your something; even more so, make no excuses that will prohibit your healing. Somethings will come and go; what will endure, however, is the memory of how you handled your something. Thus, I pray:

> Help us, Lord, to identify our somethings—those cancers present in our lives. Give us the courage to look inward, the strength to acknowledge the discovery, and the willingness to surrender our infirmities into your capable, healing hands. We're tired of tripping, Father. We're weary from the toll that our cancers have exacted upon us, not just within our flesh but also in regards to our faith. Keep us in your healing grace until all of our somethings fade into nothings and health returns to our souls. Amen.

Living Forward

- Take time to consider your "something." Name it, and examine it in light of the American Cancer Society's definition of cancer. Do you have cancer? Think broadly to include all manner of invasions to your soul and body that are seeking to destroy a healthy lifestyle.

- Why is personal suffering sometimes minimized? What benchmark do you use to measure suffering?

- Review the following scriptures, and record the somethings of the particular individuals involved. What encouragement can you draw from their witness?
    - Luke 22:39–46
    - Luke 22:54–62
    - 2 Corinthians 11:16–12:1

5

Everybody Has a Story

Now it is required that those who have been given a trust must prove faithful.
—1 Corinthians 4:2

THE COMPUTER DOCTOR stopped by my house last Saturday. He's been faithful to make house calls since our moving here last year. We've certainly had our fair share of technical maladies, my laptop being the latest victim. It was in rare form the day the doctor came by, on display and more than willing to unleash its temperamental side. The subsequent irritation of the doctor was obvious to me; I kept apologizing for the problem. He kept reassuring me that he had the answer. An hour later, the problem was solved, at least, temporarily.

The doctor was quick to make his way to the door; after all, it was a Saturday. I asked him about his willingness to work on the weekends. He told me that he worked all the time, even on Sundays. When I commented about his "really liking his work," he stopped his forward progression, leaned back on the door frame, and began to tell me a story—his story.

Five years earlier, he had lost his wife in a car accident. His fifteen-year-old son was the driver of the vehicle; a maneuver to overcorrect the wheel threw their Pontiac into oncoming traffic. The boy's mother was killed, and the son was left with a tremendous grief . . . a lasting burden. His father's grief remains as well. I heard it in his voice. I saw it in his eyes—tears raw and fresh and pouring forth from a gaping wound that was not yet healed. We spent some time talking about that wound, reliving that painful memory, and working on some sorrow that apparently had been simmering just beneath the surface of his perpetual busyness.

Funny how that happens—the doing of daily work and then, without notice, the working out of extended grief. I got the feeling that the doc doesn't share his pain with most folks. On the exterior, he's a tough guy, a retired veteran spending his retirement years tinkering around with computers. I don't imagine he came to my house expecting to shed some tears. I certainly didn't expect them. Yet they arrived because a single question triggered a response from somewhere deep within him, a "something" that obviously is a big thing for the doctor. And I started thinking about his pain, his suffering, his something.

If everybody has something, then everybody has a story attached to their something. Every hard season, every malignancy growing in a heart, mind, and soul comes with a script, with real characters reading real lines against the backdrop of real scenery, all within the context of real living. Good stories consist of real stories. Your story, my story, the computer doctor's story—all of them belonging to each of us and to the world, for we are real people, living in real times. And for life to make sense, for survivorship to happen, for the continuation of humanity, and for the betterment of our hearts, we must be willing to share our stories with one another, to open up about our somethings and to allow others a word or two of witness regarding our forward progression.

This is how we survive our lean seasons. This is a catalyst for moving forward beyond our somethings. With the telling of our stories comes personal development. Shared words push us onward, at least a few steps beyond the point of our last painful prod. Stories are a powerful tool for healing. We add to our understanding as we take in the stories of others and as we tell our stories in return.

I have a story; it's taken forty-five years to write it. The latest chapter is called "Cancer." It won't be my final chapter—that one will write its witness long after I've made it home to Jesus. But this chapter, perhaps more than the other chapters in my life, will be lengthier, will have a few more words included in it, not because they're more worthy than the other words that have been written but because there has been a hefty price tag attached to their release. My cancer chapter has been a costly inclusion. Still, it is there in bold ink, and it cannot be deleted.

It can be ignored, go unspoken and unwritten by me in hopes that omission will silence its impact. But disregard for my cancer's presence doesn't mean it doesn't exist. It simply means that I am unwilling to allow it to be a conduit for change in myself and in the lives of those who choose to enter into my story. I believe that all of my days have been ordained for me by God, including the cancer ones. Accordingly, he's entrusted me with the living out of them, the surviving beyond them, and the telling therein. God has not allowed me this something for nothing. There is eternal value beneath its tough exterior.

Everybody Has a Story

My cancer is a sacred trust. And while I do not believe God has authored my suffering, I do believe he allowed it into my story because he knows I love him and that I will not walk away from him, despite my pain. He knows that I was and still am and will always be his child, no matter the somethings that interject their witness into my life.

I don't know how my story is reading in this season. Some days it's all I can do to just get through the day, keeping my something at a low simmer. Some days my cancer gets the best of me and life lives at a full-on boil. But every now and again, I get really close to getting it right—to opening up my story for the world to read and to living up to the trust I've been given by God. Those are the days when I feel the Father's rich favor, and I know that my life is unfolding in accordance with his will—a will not rooted in suffering for suffering's sake but that allows me the privilege of suffering for the kingdom's sake.

Oh, the stories we're writing! Even more so, the stories that are writing us. Who can fathom the depth and witness of your book that will one day be on the shelf alongside the books of our spiritual ancestors and forever be a living, eternal word? How is your story reading these days? You've got one, you know—a narrative worth sharing. A story entrusted to your capable, God-shaped heart.

Live it like you mean it, tell it like you know it, and never be afraid to allow your something a chapter or two of strong witness alongside the other chapters of your life. Courageous is the one who leaves ample paper for the penning of suffering seasons. Thus, I pray:

Give us courage, Lord, to write our stories; grant us wisdom and strength for the pens that now reside in our hands. Guide us to write the words that are buried deep within our hearts. Our stories are exactly that . . . ours. No one else can claim them; no one else can live them. You have entrusted us with their telling. Keep us truthful, keep us faithful, and above all, keep us mindful of the chapters you have entrusted to our safekeeping. Humbly we receive them all, and with your help, we will endeavor to gracefully live them for your sake and for the good of your kingdom. Amen.

Living Forward

☙ What story has God entrusted you with in this season?

Beyond the Scars: Daring to Live Forward

- What earlier chapters in your life have prepared your heart for the penning of this current one?

- How does your story "read" to others? With grace and faith or with distrust and confusion? What message are you sending?

- In the face of certain death, the following saints lived their "somethings" with the courage and conviction of their faith. Read these scriptures, and record any ways their stories infuse hope into your struggle:

  - Daniel 3:13–30
  - Esther 4:12–17
  - Acts 6:8–15; 7:54–60

6

Taking Good Care of Your Heart

What you heard from me, keep as the pattern of sound teaching, with faith and love in Christ Jesus. Guard the good deposit that was entrusted to you—guard it with the help of the Holy Spirit who lives in you.

—2 Timothy 1:13–14

SHE SLID MY book proposal back in my direction. A lump rose in my throat as moistness collected in the corners of my eyes. The acquisitions editor from a major publishing house was rejecting my work . . . again.

"Cancer doesn't sell; I can't get my publishing board to take on works like yours."

I held my tongue. What I wanted to say was, "Cancer does sell . . . just ask the 1.5 million individuals who will be added as cancer statistics this year. Ask them if they need a faith-based resource to serve as a companion for their journey." But I didn't say it; instead, I just thanked the editor for her time and turned to leave. As I did, she asked me a final question.

"Tell me something. How did you do it? How were you able to embrace your cancer season rather than retreat from it?"

My heart swelled with joy. While I wouldn't be able to leave her with a copy of my book proposal, I would be allowed to leave her with something better: the truth.

"Faith deposits," I said. "Years and years worth of intentional investments into my spiritual bank account. That's the single reason behind my being able to handle my cancer season. I've been taking care of my heart for a long time. God and I go way back. The work we've done together in my yesterdays has been the underpinning for my today. Be sure and take good care of your heart. Be sure to do so under the watchful gaze of the cross."

"Take good care of your heart." A few words of benediction I've been known to use as a way of ending common conversations. They are words that issue from my personal reservoir of truth—from practical life experience. The meaning of my declaration is not always clear to those on the receiving end. Some conclude that I'm referencing the hollow, muscular organ in charge of their blood circulation. That's not the definition I'm after, not really. Certainly, cardiovascular health is an important message to relay, but even more so is the recommendation regarding the development of our spiritual health—the fitness of our faith. When filtered through these lenses, heart health is taken to another level. Taking care of our hearts to lay hold of eternal truth supersedes temporal need.

Why not just a "good-bye" or "talk to you soon" when finishing my conversations? Why not something safer, more generic, and less intrusive? Because this season of cancer has underscored for me the critical importance of making faith deposits into my heart's bank account before the suffering withdrawals begin. The faith that you and I are willing to work on today—the deliberate acts of strengthening our spiritual hearts and shoring up faith's borders—will serve as a strong anchor for us when tomorrow's winds of adversity howl their menace.

Cancer has given me permission to write these words of recommendation to you, for I am a woman who has been challenged to courageously live them out in this last year. My test of faith began on August 23, 2010. Together, my husband and I sat hand in hand in my doctor's office, awaiting word regarding a recent biopsy performed on my right breast. Two weeks earlier, a routine mammogram came back inconclusive, which led to an ultrasound, which eventually led to a biopsy under the watchful and careful eye of a breast surgeon.

On this day, she entered the room with her perfunctory greeting, and then she got down to business. "Mrs. Olsen, the results of your biopsy indicate the presence of a cancerous tumor—invasive ductal carcinoma, the most common type of breast cancer experienced in women—"

Forgive me for not remembering how she finished her sentence. In fact, I didn't allow her to finish her thought. Instead, I raised my hand to her and said, "You need to stop here. Do you realize the words that you have just spoken over me?"

Tenderly, she acknowledged that, in fact, she did realize her harsh indictment, and then she paused long enough for me to take it in. My husband's ashen expression indicated to me that he wasn't taking the news very well. Realizing his limited usefulness in that moment, I quickly turned back to the doctor and simply asked, "What's next then? Where do we go from here?"

Taking Good Care of Your Heart

Where we went from there was forward to a six-month, chosen suffering that included MRIs, PET scans, CT scans, MUGA scans, countless vials of bloodwork, more biopsies of the left breast, a double mastectomy, port-placement surgery, eight rounds of chemotherapy, and a hysterectomy, to finally conclude with a low-dose chemo, estrogen-blocking pill to be taken daily over the next five years. It was an exhaustive, thorough, painful walk-through toward healing, suffering withdrawals of the deepest kind.

In contrast, there have been many good moments, important life lessons, and rich perspectives afforded to me because of my cancer journey. I've been able to receive them instead of backing away from them because of the faith deposits I've consistently made into my heart's spiritual bank account over the years. My previously rehearsed faith has been a worthy, life-saving investment and has allowed me a rich measure of peace in the midst of this trial. There is no other justification, rationalization, or explanation that can be given for the holy confidence I've managed to hold on to, despite all the ways cancer has chipped away at my faith reserves. Without a hefty surplus of faith on the front side of my cancer, getting through it with any measure of grace and understanding was an unlikely prospect.

It is the same for us as we travel through our "somethings." In her book *Anonymous*, Alicia Chole has this to say about faith investments prior to suffering's witness: "Trials tell us less about our future than they do about our past. Why? Because the decisions we make in difficult places today are greatly the product of decisions we made in the unseen places of our yesterdays."[2]

"The unseen places of our yesterdays . . ." In the realm of tomorrow's unfolding, yesterday is really today—a good day for heart investments. And so I tell you again what I've been telling others, and even more so, myself, "Take good care of your heart." Don't wait until tomorrow's trials to start your regimen toward heart health. Begin today by making personal deposits of your time and energy into an exercise routine that will strengthen and fortify your faith for the road ahead. The investment you willingly make today will be the strengthened understanding of your tomorrows.

On August 22, 2010, I had no idea what would be the outcome of my August 23, but I had a strong inclination regarding the final results. Rather than fainting with worry or fighting the possibilities, I simply bowed my heart and my knees and prayed the prayer I've been carrying around with me from my earliest days. It carries me still, and it will finish me home. Perhaps you need the eternal witness of its reminder this day. Thus, I pray (see Matt. 6:9–13):

Our Father, who art in heaven, hallowed be thy name.
Thy kingdom come, Thy will be done,
On earth as it is in heaven.
Give us this day, our daily bread,
And forgive us our debts as we forgive our debtors,
Lead us not into temptation, but deliver us from evil.
For Thine is the kingdom, and the power, and the glory forever. Amen.

Living Forward

- Are you taking care of your heart? If so, how? If not, why not?

- Using the analogy of cardiovascular health, what parallels can you draw to the importance of spiritual heart health?

- When has your previously rehearsed faith served as a strong anchor for you in a time of trial and testing?

- Read the following scriptures, and record how the early Christians invested in their faith. What common thread runs throughout?

  - Acts 2:42–47
  - Acts 4:23–26; 32–37
  - Acts 5:12–16

7

Living Up to Your Learning

Do your best to present yourself to God as one approved, a workman who does not need to be ashamed and who correctly handles the word of truth.
—2 Timothy 2:15

MR. ROBERTS WAS a scary fellow, prone to strong emotion, a struggling artist obviously frustrated by the fact that his creativity was constrained by his reality—his occupation as an English teacher at my county high school. Sitting beneath his tutelage touched on my insecurities as a fledgling teenager trying to fit into a social scene that was more content to leave me as I was—unnoticed. I was more than content to remain unseen by Mr. Roberts. Receiving his attention usually indicated his displeasure in something I had done or failed to do. It was tough being a student in his classroom.

That is, until the day when he read aloud a portion of a paper I had written and boldly proclaimed, "Now that's how you write, students." He turned to me, his eyes bulging with excitement, and placed the paper on my desk. "Excellent work, Elaine."

I was embarrassed by his acknowledgement but not enough to douse the joy I felt inside. Mr. Roberts had noticed my words; in doing so, he stirred up a confidence in me that would move me forward to more fully explore my love for writing. I am grateful for his acknowledgement and for the difficult responsibility of being his student.

It's hard being a student in the classroom of a temperamental teacher, but sometimes it proffers good results. Mr. Roberts was my test case; cancer, perhaps, is my hardest one. Of all the classrooms I've sat in throughout my lifetime—grade school through high school, college, graduate school, life school (the learning that only comes about through practical life experience)—out of all these, I don't suppose there has been one that has required more of me than the classroom I sit in today, under the teacher named *cancer*. None of them have necessitated my undivided attention as much as she.

Like Mr. Roberts, she's not always been kind; rarely is she in a good mood. Most days, I don't understand her language, and her grading scale isn't always in keeping with fair standards. She's sent me to the corner a time or two . . . the woodshed as well. She's never won any teacher-of-the-year awards or been bombarded with students' requests to sign their yearbooks. But one thing is certain: cancer has been thorough in her instruction. She refuses to skip over chapters, and she doesn't seem in any hurry to finish the curriculum. She's pushy, persistent, and willing to pursue me on days when I am not as willing to be her student. Cancer has never backed down from the lectern, but there have been moments when I've backed away from her tutelage.

Early on in my diagnosis, I wrote this bold statement of faith: "Cancer will not be my undoing; rather it will be the threshold of my emerging." It's easy to make bold statements of faith prior to suffering's arrival. Casually spoken faith not yet tempered by trials will most likely receive a thorough examination under the microscope of practical life experiences. This has certainly been the case with me.

As my trial began, I knew I had a decision to make—bow out of cancer's classroom and find my bitterness, or bow low, lean into my learning with the hopes of becoming a better version of me. To get there required a three-step process, a course of study for all who desire to (as we say in the South) "make our grade" and advance on to higher learning. Teachable students are those who *show up* to the classroom, *listen up* to the teacher, and *live up* to their learning.

Any shortcutting this process will likely leave us as we are or, worse, turn us into a version of ourselves that we never intended to be.

Showing up to the classroom means choosing the confines of a desk over the comfort of a bed. It means taking a shower, getting out of our pajamas, packing a lunch, stepping onto the bus, and maybe even walking those two miles our parents talked about because we understand the importance of a day's learning. Getting the notes from a friend isn't the same as being there, especially in our classrooms of suffering; some notes are best penned by our own hands. But it's not enough just to show up to the classroom. I've been in many classrooms where the pupils around me were zoned out, looking out the window, or sleeping their way through the lesson. No, if we really want to make our grade, we need to be willing to move further into the learning process.

We need to *listen up* to the teacher. We may not like her; perhaps she wasn't our pick for this semester, but those of us who are teachable are wise enough to realize that the greatest learning often filters through the hands of a hard teacher. Accordingly, we get a

Living Up to Your Learning

good night's sleep before the school day begins; we grab some protein on the way out the door and come prepared with pen and paper to record this teacher's every word. Cancer has had a great many things to say to me in the last year. I'm glad I took notes and listened up to her lectures. In doing so, I have a textbook filled with references that will allow me to move into the third step of the learning process—*living up* to my learning.

Living up to our learning means that we study hard for the test, take the test, and receive a passing grade. I've never seen cancer give a 100 percent on any test she's given. But I've witnessed a lot of, "above average." A lot of, "Now that's how you write, students!" For learning truly to be learning, we must apply the lessons of the classroom to our everyday lives. To forget the test material is to waste the hours logged in the chair. We live up to our learning by investing our knowledge, insight, and understanding into the lives of others. This doesn't give them permission to forego their own classrooms; it simply means that we freely offer insight and encouragement to them as they struggle to make their grade.

This is part and parcel of why I'm writing this book—to offer some insight from my time in cancer's classroom and to encourage you as you struggle through yours. I know how hard it is to be her student, but I also know how rewarding it is to make my grade. When I push my learning aside—bury it and keep it as history rather than as ministry—well, that's just playing around with the truth. And the truth is, cancer is one of the best teachers I've ever had.

What classroom are you sitting in today? What roll call includes your name? What chair rests beneath your intention for learning? We all woke up to a classroom's requirement—a desk, a teacher, a chalkboard, and a lesson plan—a day's worth of growing our minds and our hearts if we are willing to be taught. Most of us will take to our learning, show up to the classroom, and invest some energy into the education process. But not everyone will make it to school on time. A few will call in sick; perhaps a few will even face jail for their willing truancy. School isn't optional for students who want to advance beyond the first grade. School is the daily privilege given to all God's children who plan on graduating with honors.

It's time we all started living up to our learning, regardless of the teacher who's taking attendance. *Show up, listen up,* and then by God's grace and empowering strength, *live up,* students. There's a world waiting to reap the benefits of your hard-fought learning. I will endeavor to do the same. Thus, I pray:

Wake us up, Lord, and get us moving toward the classroom this day. Shake the dust from our eyes and the complacency from our hearts so that we might receive the benefit from sitting inside the walls of our struggling seasons. Jesus, you've read the syllabus ahead of time, and you know what will be required of us. You too sat under a hard teacher, the cross. You now strengthen us with your learning through your witness and through your Word. You lived up so that we might live up as well. Thank you for showing us how to make our grade, even when the requirements seem too much. Amen.

Living Forward

- What classroom are you sitting in today? Name the teacher and describe the syllabus and the students sitting with you.

- What are some of the hardest lessons you are learning in this season? What worthiness is attached to those lessons?

- Which part of the learning process is most difficult for you: *showing up* to the classroom, *listening up* to the teacher, or *living up* to your learning? Explain.

- Reflect on Moses' struggle in regards to his learning as reflected in Exodus 2–5. What were some of the obstacles he faced under the teacher named *deliverance*? Read Deuteronomy 30:11–20, and reflect on some of Moses' closing remarks to the children of Israel. What primary life lesson did he learn because of his struggles?

8

Real Love Looks Beyond the Scars

*Therefore we do not lose heart. Though outwardly we are wasting away,
yet inwardly we are being renewed day by day.*
—2 Corinthians 4:16

QUIETLY WE WAITED for her, our hearts tethered together in a way we'd never felt throughout our thirteen years of marriage. Few words were spoken between us. They seemed less necessary in those moments, almost intrusive. Instead, we just looked at one another, knowing that our lives were about to take another turn—a reality we had known was coming, yet were not adequately prepared for: the look of my new body.

Three weeks earlier, we'd sat in these same chairs, hearing my diagnosis for the first time—breast cancer. A lot of history had passed between that day and this one, a lot of firsts and lasts, a lot of holding on to the past, and a lot of letting go of it in order to live in the present.

Even now, some ten months beyond when the carnage began, it really hasn't sunk in—the fullness of what I've experienced. Memories get tangled up with my emotions, and raw emotions rarely allow the release of reasoned responses, written or otherwise. That being said, my memory is crystal clear regarding this particular September morning—the day when I would take a look at the wounding I had willingly chosen just nine days earlier—the amputation of my breasts.

Tenderly, nurse Beth unwrapped my dressings. Beneath the bandages was a week-long, hidden mystery—a fright I had refused to address in the days preceding its unveiling.

It wasn't as hideous as I had imagined it would be. Instead, it simply was what it is—a new version of me, packaged differently, in an old flesh.

My husband and I shed tears. I knew that we would. And when I looked into his eyes, I saw something I hadn't thought was possible. I saw a deeper love looking back at me—a renewed love—a love that courageously took my heart yet again as his own and silently reaffirmed to me that I was his bride of choice.

Thirteen years earlier, he professed his love to me on our wedding day. I remember the early-morning walk I took with my father prior to the day's festivities. Few words passed between us as we paced our way around town; some walks don't require much conversation, just a respect for the gift of being together. But toward the end of our stroll, Dad spoke a few words anyway. I think he knew I, as a single mother of two young sons about to enter into a second marriage, needed to hear them. Dad's gentle words of encouragement seeded calmness within my anxious heart. In speaking them to me, my dad gave me a blessing—a fatherly validation regarding the vows that I was about to make to my man.

"Elaine, today you are marrying Billy every bit as much for your boys as you are for yourself; in doing so, you are giving them a gift. You are allowing them to witness how a man is supposed to love a woman."

My father's words are as clear to me today as they were back then. They served as a strong anchor for me in the years that followed, when the intermittent winds of marital strife threatened to destroy previously spoken vows. They still anchor me today. My dad was right. And while Billy hasn't always loved me perfectly, he's always been perfectly willing to try. He's never given up on me, our marriage, and the life we have built together with our four children.

My husband loves me, and I love him. On that September morning in the doctor's office, we celebrated the gift of life, both his and mine. It happened to be his birthday, and while there weren't any gifts for him to unwrap, he told me that he had just unwrapped the most precious gift he'd ever been given—me. He told me that I was enough of a gift and that he didn't need wrappings and bows. He just needed me, the new version of me. I was his birthday blessing.

That moment between us was one of the sweetest, most tender deposits of love I have ever received as a human being, even sweeter than the love I have experienced as a daughter and as a mother. Why? It is because my husband's love for me is a chosen love, not a love out of obligation. There isn't a familial blood connection to link our hearts, just a willingness to dig in, hold on, and stay the course, despite the lean seasons that come

Real Love Looks Beyond the Scars

our way. I am grateful for the bittersweet reality of that moment because it reminds me of an eternal truth too easily forgotten when life lives easily and love is taken for granted.

Real love—a God-intended kind of love—looks beyond the scars to celebrate the life that resides beneath. Real love chooses the heart above the flesh, the commitment above the suffering, the "I will" above the "I won't," the "I do" above the "I don't." Real love cries real tears, holds trembling hands, and refuses to look the other way, even when a harsh wounding leaves a hideous scar. That kind of loving isn't rooted in fairy tales or feel-good chick flicks. No, that kind of loving is rooted in God. It authors with him, extends through him, and is sustained by him because of the enabling work of the cross.

Calvary is the benchmark for real love. Calvary holds the standard for willing wounds, chosen suffering, and sacred scarring all in the name of love . . . all for the cause of life, for birthday upon birthday that unwraps and reveals a new version of us, packaged differently, in an old flesh. We get a new heart to replace an aging one and a stronger faith to supplant a fledgling one.

Jesus Christ is the righteous standard—our best opportunity to witness how a Savior is supposed to love a sinner. He has loved us perfectly. He loves us still. Christ's love—a God-intended kind of love—looks beyond our scars to celebrate the life that resides beneath. Today, he's asking the same of us, to look beyond his scars and to take hold of the life and love that reside beneath. What tender, beautiful, redeeming grace! Thus, I pray:

> *Unwrap me, Lord, even as I unwrap you. May the exchange of love between us not be a reminder of all things lost, but rather a celebration of everything gained. May the silence spoken between us reaffirm the vows we have made to each other. Yours is an everlasting, unconditional, grace-filled, perfect love. Forgive me when mine falls short, and show me how to love the most excellent way. "I will" and "I do" for the rest of my days. Amen.*

Living Forward

ଔ Describe the scars that remain from your recent wounding. Why is it difficult to view them in front of others?

Beyond the Scars: Daring to Live Forward

ଔ Who has loved you beyond your scars—looked past your wounding to take hold of the life that resides beneath?

ଔ Consider Christ's scars by reading the following scriptures:

- Isaiah 49:15–16
- Isaiah 53:1–5
- Matthew 27:27–44

ଔ How does Christ's willing suffering better enable you to deal with yours?

9

God Keeps Pace with Your Pain

He withdrew about a stone's throw beyond them, knelt down and prayed, "Father if you are willing take this cup from me; yet, not my will but yours be done." An angel appeared to him and strengthened him.
—Luke 22:41–43

I PULLED HER e-mail out of my three-ring binder—the cancer binder. I've kept many notes of kindness and encouragement that surfaced early on with my diagnosis. I knew there would come a look-back day, a time when I would more fully reflect on the ministry of sentiments written by friends. Today was her day; the e-mail wasn't randomly selected. Rather, it was remembered. It meant that much to me upon my first receiving it. It means a great deal to me today; thus, I gave it a second glance.

Her e-mail arrived in my inbox on the eve of my mastectomy. Her words were, in part, a response to a reflection I had written about my upcoming surgery. In that reflection, I talked about my desire for a deeper intimacy with God that might not have come to me had cancer's suffering road not been my allowance. My friend knows something of suffering. In recent years, she's carried a heavy grief over the loss of her daughter. I trust her words, because I trust her heart. Hearts shaped by God through painful seasons are hearts that can be relied upon for the truth. This was hers given to me that day:

This morning as I drove to my hair appointment, I was thinking about you. I felt that, even though you are a woman of great faith and have a strong spiritual walk, you are going to see God in a way you've never seen him before . . . something new that will change you. You are going to be taken to a place with God that you've never been before and see him as you've never seen him. There are some places, Elaine, where only you and God can go to together. Others will want to come along for the ride, but they won't understand. Only God will.

Only God. As much as I didn't want her to be right, as much as I shuddered at the thought of the extreme isolation that her truth forecast for me, she was accurate in her predictions, not because it was her truth but rather because it was God's. He used my friend to speak both blessing and caution to my heart that day. She risked something with the sharing—my misunderstanding. But I didn't misunderstand her. I already held some sobering expectations regarding my upcoming road. I just didn't want the uncertainty of it all, and I certainly didn't want the pain required to help me "see God in a way I'd never seen him before." Surely there had to be an easier way, a shorter path to sacred revelation.

That was then; this is now, and I have seen God in a way I'd never seen him before. Together we've traveled to unseen vistas and to knee-deep intimacy as the hours stretched into days, days into weeks, and the weeks calendered into months. Ten of them now, filled with many moments of wrestling out my heart's faith before the loving Father who created it. Days of questions without answers. Hour upon hour of sleepless nights, where pain was my portion and tears my comfort. Times when I felt forgotten, times when I knew I was remembered. Very few emotional highs and an ample collection of extreme lows. And it was in those dark periods of deep-soul searching when the fullness of my friend's words came back around to me as strength. They carried me through to hope.

Apparently there *wasn't* an easier way or a shorter route to seeing God in a way I'd never seen him before. Suffering would be the path to take me there, and only God was able to move me past my confusion. For the perspective and understanding now afforded to my heart, for the discovery of those vistas, and for the blessing of soul-stirring intimacy shared with the Father, I can lift my hands toward heaven and say, "Thank you, God, for allowing me this journey. Thank you for keeping pace with my pain."

God keeps pace with our pain, even when no one else does, when no one else can. He best understands the requirement of a willing suffering because he required no less of his Son. Jesus journeyed to a garden wrestling and then to the requirement of the cross—a place reserved for him and his Father. No one else understood the fullness of that surrender until it was finished. And as I read it in hindsight, as I see the story unfold on the pages of Scripture, I am deeply grateful for the harder way and the longer route that my Savior willingly embraced so that I can know him in a way I've never known him before.

God Keeps Pace with Your Pain

Had Christ not done what his Father sent him to do, my suffering and yours would have no eternal value. Without Calvary, our "somethings" are nothing more than burdens to be endured. When we approach our pain without kingdom perspective, we rely on quick fixes. We search for the shortest route between our suffering and its release. But with kingdom perspective, we willingly cede the shortest route to the road that includes a King's companionship. When we do so, something changes in us. Something new moves in to replace the old, and eyes once blinded by temporal understanding are opened up to see with eternal perspective—a place to which only God can lead us.

At this point in my journey, I don't imagine I've seen the fullness of all God wants to reveal to me on this side of eternity. With every new day and each new trust I'm given, I'm challenged to relinquish my easiest and shortest inclinations to an eternal preference that stays focused on God's greater gain. It's not usually what I want to do, but it's the best thing I can possibly do. More than any other blessing I may gain on this earth, what I desire the most is to know God, see God, hear God, and live God. And then out of that knowing, seeing, hearing, and living, I want to lead others to know, see, hear, and live accordingly. If suffering is the road that takes me there, then suffering is worth the surrender.

Today is your look-back day, friends. You may not have a three-ring binder filled with encouraging e-mails from kindred friends, but you have God's encouraging words contained within your Bible. Those words speak eternally, never losing the power of their witness. If you are in a season of suffering and feeling all alone, know that God and only God is the one person capable of keeping pace with your pain. There are some places where only the two of you can travel together. It just may be the most beautiful, unseen vista of your earthly tenure. It's certainly been mine. Thus, I pray:

Grant us courage to walk in isolation with you, Father, all the way through to our something new. Keep us from shortcutting the process that will take us there. You have so much more for us to know, see, and hear, and to show us how to live according to your plans for our lives. We pray for more faith to believe in those plans and then to confidently walk them with you as our faithful guide. Thank you for remembering me in my suffering and for instilling the promise of morning light into a dark-night wrestling. You are my Savior, and today, I concede my saving to you. Amen.

Living Forward

- In what ways has your knowledge of God and intimacy with God grown during your suffering?

- Do you agree or disagree that there are some places where only you and God can go to together? Explain.

- Read the following scenes from Jesus' life that mirror this idea of isolation with God. What are some of the benefits of Christ's being tested in isolation? What are some possible pitfalls?

    - Matthew 4:1–11
    - Matthew 26:36–46

- What encouragement do you receive from Christ's experience?

10
Suffering Need Needs a Suffering Friend

Do your best to come to me quickly, for Demas, because he loved this world, has deserted me.... Only Luke is with me.
—2 Timothy 4:9–11

THE WORDS FROM his pen haunt me now, even though nearly two thousand years have passed since they were first inked into parchment.

"Only Luke . . ."

Two words that pen a vivid portrait of comfort and pain, all from the same inkwell. Comfort because to have a "Luke," especially in times of intense suffering, is a rich extension of heavenly grace. Pain because to have only one Luke in such seasons seems hardly enough. It seems to me there should have been more Lukes to stand beside and sit beneath the weightiness of Paul's suffering—at least a few of them. Suffering seasons can be lonely isolations, thus the plea from Paul's pen to Timothy, "Do your best to come to me quickly."

Suffering need needs a suffering friend. Not just any friend, but a friend who has walked a similar road. Friends who are willing to enter into our struggles—who sit with us among our chains, our separations, and our ashes—do so because they understand the sacred value of having a Luke in the midst of trials. Most likely, those friends have been the beneficiaries of a Luke friendship at some point in their own journeys, and now they are paying it forward to others in need. They willingly extend comforting companionship to suffering souls because they have received a similar portion in their own times of hardship.

Paul speaks to this comforting exchange in 2 Corinthians 1:3–5: "Praise be to the God and Father of our Lord Jesus Christ, the Father of compassion and the God of all comfort, who comforts us in all our troubles, so that we can comfort those in any trouble with the comfort we ourselves have received from God. For just as the sufferings of Christ flow over into our lives, so also through Christ our comfort overflows."

I've been privileged to receive Christ's comfort from many cancer friends during my time of treatment. Several friends preceded my diagnosis: Maxine, Marilyn, Beth, and Carol—my Bible-study girls who willingly allowed me a ringside seat to their suffering. They showed me how to live each day with purpose, with laughter, and with God's kindness as the standard. They didn't keep the hideous side of their cancer from me; instead, they allowed me its truth. In doing so, they prepared me for the eventual reality that would make me one of them—a cancer patient. And although they didn't know about my cancer before they made their walks home to heaven, God knew. How grateful I am for the gift of God's heavenly witness given to me through them.

I've also had the honor of living my cancer alongside many others who are walking a similar path. Valiantly, they are facing the realities of our disease and forging onward to take hold of their healing. Although most of them were strangers to me prior to my diagnosis, they have willingly entered into my story as I have entered into theirs. We are a family of sorts, living out our struggles before one another and receiving each other's pain without question. The connections we share would not have been possible but for the disease that drew us together. There is comfort in numbers, and I am blessed to be numbered alongside these friends. All of them, past and present, have been Luke to me, but none more so than the Luke named Judith.

Judith and I have never met face-to-face, yet I count her as a kindred friend. She's been a reader at my website for a few years now. Early on, she wrote to me about her cancer, her sustained struggle for the better part of ten years. I suppose she's had more surgeries, more hospitalizations, more treatments using a wide variety of medicines than many of us combined. Judith has been a constant friend and mentor to me, willing to dispense the comfort of Christ that she has known. She is an extension of God's loving heart to this world, making hefty deposits into my own heart long before I received my diagnosis.

No wonder she was the second person I called after hearing my news. Her response was strong; her love all the more. Over the past year, she's come alongside me in a way other friends haven't been able to, not because they didn't want to but because they didn't have firsthand knowledge of this dreaded disease. Judith has been my cell mate in these past months. Day and night, she's been available to tackle my questions, to bandage my

Suffering Need Needs a Suffering Friend

pain, to add comfort to my confusion; I like to think I've done the same for her—a holy exchange between two suffering hearts.

She, my Luke; I, her Paul. I, her Luke; she, my Paul. Comforting comfort of the heavenly kind! Perhaps you've experienced a similar portion. If you've ever walked the suffering road, then I imagine you've had a Luke or two to come alongside you in your struggles. I certainly pray that's been the case. Suffering need needs a suffering friend.

I don't know where you are today—whether there's a "something" that's eating away at you and keeping you from experiencing certain healing. But this one thing I do know: our pain belongs to one another. It is a gift we give to each other. God never intended for us to go it alone in this world. He intends for us to extend comfort to others out of the comfort we have received from his willing surrender to the cross. When we get that—when we understand God's investment strategy as it pertains to our personal pain—then hell's determined purpose is vanquished, and victory belongs to the King.

Tomorrow is another day to live your kingdom assignment. Someone will cross your path who needs the love and commitment of a Luke. Be that Luke. And should you ever be the one in need, never fear to ask for more. Speak your need to our Father, and then, in turn, speak your need to his saints. If there's one thing I've been privileged to experience throughout the course of my cancer, it has been the unmerited, lavish love of God through his people, his Lukes. Never have I known it to be so strong, so long, so wide, so high, and so deep. It stretches across my soul this day to comfort me and to carry me through to tomorrow. Thus, I pray:

Thank you, Father, for the Lukes you have given to me. They have prepared my heart for the road I am walking, and they strengthen my feet and faith for the journey I'm continuing. Thank you for seeing my need before it ever arrived upon the soil of my life and for making sure that I had the suffering witness of my Bible-study girls. I am grateful for the survivors who stand with me today and for my cell mate, Judith, who has cried tender tears and prayed holy prayers on my behalf. Together, all of us have shaken the gates of hell with the strong and determined truth of heaven. One day soon, we will all be together at home with you, our suffering long gone and our sure healing on display, to the glory of your name. Even so, keep us to the road of our comforting today. Amen.

Living Forward

- Who has served as a "Luke" to you in your suffering? In what ways has his or her personal pain served as a catalyst to ministering to your pain?

- Why is it important to have a Luke who has walked a similar road as yours?

- Read Paul's account of his imprisonments in 2 Timothy 4:9–18 and Acts 16:16–36. What role of encouragement did Paul's friends play in his survivorship?

- What two or three people is God calling you to come alongside to serve as an encouragement to them in their time of struggle?

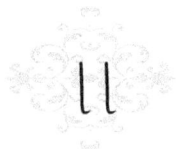

11

Making an Apology to Suffering

I consider that our present sufferings are not worth comparing with the glory that will be revealed in us.

—Romans 8:18

MAKE YOUR APOLOGY to suffering. Go ahead. Tell it you're sorry; tell it you regret ever thinking that it was less than what it really is. Confess your ignorance, and admit that you were wrong in your assumption that suffering really isn't worthy of all the press it receives.

It is worthy and deserving of respect. Just ask anyone who is suffering.

Merriam-Webster defines *suffering* as "pain."[3] That's it—a one-word description. What do we do with a definition like this? Is that really all it is—pain? If that's the case, then I imagine every one of us could add a witness regarding suffering's intrusion into our lives. I'm not sure how our sufferings weigh out in comparison, if somewhere there's a scale on the market to rank personal pain. What I do believe to be true is what I've said before. If your "something" is tripping you up, then it deserves your respect; it deserves mine as well, no matter how big or small your something might seem to the rest of the world.

Suffering is a respectable tenet of our human existence. It is to be expected, not denied, and esteemed, not pitied. And while it comes to us in varying degrees at different seasons in our lives, it is easily identifiable because of the pain attached to its arrival. Sometimes suffering is minimal in its witness, sometimes more enduring, but all the time, it is painful.

Beyond the Scars: Daring to Live Forward

Over the course of my painful season, I've thought a great deal about my friend Marilyn and her suffering, about her courageous fight against cancer and all the many ways she chose to deal with her disease. I've thought about her choices, her responses, the days she chose isolation over population, the times she seemed to push *away from* instead of pushing *into* those of us who loved her—those of us who wanted to do more for her than to simply sit by and watch her slip away home to Jesus.

It seemed reasonable to me that she'd want me around. After all, I was laughter and smiles and hope for tomorrow. All I wanted to do was help—a seemingly reasonable and generous gift to give to someone in her time of great need. I wanted to be let in—cloistered in that inner circle that would give me safe sanctuary and open access to her pain. Instead, I was given arm's-length access to her suffering. That was enough for her; it should have been enough for me. But it wasn't. I judged, and today I render my heavenward apology to her and say, "I'm sorry for thinking that I needed more . . . for assuming that I understood, for pretending that a few words of well-spoken faith were enough to ease your discomfort, for forcing your feelings when all you really wanted to do was to hunker down, tunnel through, breathe your next breath until the next breath arrived, indicating you had made it beyond the momentary horror that gripped your flesh."

Yes, I've thought about Marilyn in recent months as I've pushed and am continuing to push my way through my own pain. I am humbled with understanding, because now I hold some of my own.

I don't wish it for any of you, not in this way. Oh, that understanding could come to us otherwise! That depth of insight could be birthed in peaceful trajectory rather than in haphazard flight. That suffering's lessons could be learned within autumn's brilliant embrace rather than winter's brittle confinement. That we could really grasp the length and breadth, height and depth of Job's renderings without ever having to scrape and spoil and sit among ashes. That we could truly learn the value of our flesh in a single pause without ever having to walk it to the outer edges of surrender. That we could hold holy truth without ever having to engage with its contrast.

Oh, that we could. Oh, that I could. Apparently, I cannot.

This time around, I must learn holy truth the hard way and confront the stinking, rotting reality of just exactly what my flesh means to me and my allegiances therein. Sorting through the layers to reach kingdom perspective, a God perspective, is moving me beyond what meets the eye and slays the flesh, and it is birthing in me something far greater than ideals and faith that stop at the front door of my heart. Such an understanding is leading me toward an unshakeable, unwavering certainty *in* and *of* the one God who can be trusted with all my days—beginning, middle, and end.

Making an Apology to Suffering

I thought I knew God before cancer. Apparently, I'd only scratched at his surface. And I am not afraid of his personal disclosure along these lines, of his willingness to draw me in and to let me see more—to ask more, to dig more, to hurt more—for I am convinced that it is in this *more* that my journey toward God really begins.

Everything prior to this season? Well, it's been nothing more than an entrée and excellent feast to whet my appetite for his Excellency. Everything next? My crossroads, the stone on my path, marking where my walkabout in faith takes a turn toward maturity. It's where I discover my kingdom story within the boundaries of God's country and when I learn the truth that I have never, ever been alone—not for a single moment.

Yes, I've thought a great deal about my friend these past few days. And in the midst of my own anguish, I've smiled a time or two, because she now holds something I've yet to fully grasp. She holds perfect understanding. She lives with holy truth. She no longer grapples with the question of her flesh because she is clothed, instead, with God's.

Indeed, it is time to make our apologies to suffering and to give it the respect it deserves. Pain is a game changer in our lives, a heart changer as well. Not that we ask for it, but as it comes—when suffering interjects its witness into our lives—we must take it seriously. It just may be the crucible that God can best use to lead us toward perfect understanding. Thus, I pray:

> *Forgive me, Lord, for ever thinking that I could get through this life without pain. Forgive me for the times when I minimized human suffering because it didn't touch me personally. My heart is overgrown with complacency. Through my suffering, unearth my calloused heart, and grow my compassion for those who suffer alongside me. Give me love where indifference resides. Give me mercy where judgment reigns. And give me understanding where ignorance abides. Use my pain to plant your kingdom seed. For your sake and for your gain, let this season not be wasted. Amen.*

Living Forward

- Reflect on a time when you've been on the outside of a loved one's suffering. How did it make you feel?

☙ How has your own pain changed your perspective regarding the way others choose to deal with theirs?

☙ What has been the worst part of your suffering? What criteria do you use in choosing those people you allow into your inner circle?

☙ Read Romans 8:18–27. What hope can be found in the midst of suffering?

12

Living Up to Your Convictions

Let us hold firmly to the faith we profess.
—Hebrews 4:14

I SAW IT in her eyes, heard it in her trembling voice. I saw it in her husband and son as well as they sat next to her during her first round of chemotherapy.

Fear, an unbridled, unrestrained worry radiating outward from an inward torment. Her fear was apparent to anyone sitting next to her, especially to those of us who've sat where she was sitting—a chemo chair. Mine happened to be located directly across from hers that day. I remember the first time I sat in one, feeling some of those same feelings of panic. I just masked mine better with conversation, laughter, and the passing out of homemade cookies. Some would call that bravery; I just called it coping—doing what I needed to do to get through those hours with some measure of peace.

A few weeks later, we sat beside one another in the chemo lounge again. This time, her countenance radiated with far less fear and more contentment. Why? I think it is because some of the mystery surrounding her treatment had been revealed. Fear of the unknown is a formidable foe on the front side of suffering. It's difficult to reason out suffering's effects until suffering has spoken its witness. Painful trials that arrive unexpectedly don't receive a lot of buildup; they just land like a bomb, exploding as unanticipated agony.

However it comes to us, whether planned or unexpected, pain can serve as a strong catalyst to paralyzing fear. I've seen it over and over again in the faces of those who are walking the cancer road with me, breaking my heart every time I witness its grip. I won't tell you that my fear is completely gone, but I'm working on it. I talk to God about it on a regular basis, confess my struggles, and ask for more of his peace, for more faith to live out my days in victory over the unknowns that await me down the road. Every day, I'm reminded of the tension that exists between faith and fear, because every day that has passed since first receiving my diagnosis, I've been reminded of a few words I bravely penned nine months earlier: "It doesn't matter how long God chooses to preserve my earthly life; what matters is how I choose to preserve him in the earthly life I've been given."

I wrote that bold statement of faith after a similar breast scare had required further tests. At the time, I fully expected the outcome would be disastrous, but it wasn't. I received a pass and then presented my bold proclamation to the world via my webpage. Nine months later, I didn't receive a pass. Cancer was my portion, and the bold statement I had earlier announced resurfaced in my heart, ringing with a clarity that sounded more like taunt than surrendered truth. *Now you get to really live this one out, Elaine. Now you have to put your money where your mouth went. Now you get to boldly live up to the faith you so bravely professed nearly a year ago.*

I was mostly prepared to live out the fullness of my convictions. Years' worth of faith investments bolstered my reserves for the hefty withdrawals about to be made. Even still, there were a few occasions of wrestling inwardly with the earlier truth I had written, especially, "It doesn't matter how long God chooses to preserve my earthly life." There were a few times when I shouted back at my previously spoken faith and said, "Yes, it does matter; I have four children, two still very young, God! And a husband I adore. Yes, it does matter! I want more days, more years, a golden anniversary. I want to die later, not now!"

And therein the bargaining began—bargains about being a better person, making a greater impact in the world for Jesus, leaving a lasting legacy that would alter the course of a future generation. You get the picture. Along these lines, I imagine you've had a few moments of holy negotiation with the Father about your "something." The carnal side of fear is the culprit, and whenever fear shouts its witness, faith is a difficult holding. Fear has the capacity to topple faith's tower in a single blow. Carnal fear has been the downfall of a great many saints. It dismantles truth and replaces it with lies.

Godly fear? Well, that's altogether different. Godly fear recognizes God for who he *is* and humbly keeps in line with his kingship. Godly fear bows to the all-knowing, all-present God, believing that he alone is able to take the somethings that are consuming us and make them into the building blocks of an extraordinary faith. Godly fear releases debilitating doubt into the capable, trustworthy hands of God, receiving in exchange his stability, his understanding, his comfort, and his peace for the journey.

Living Up to Your Convictions

It takes awhile to build a strong foundation of faith. It's far easier to write and speak about faith than it is to live it. This doesn't mean that our proclamations of faith are null and void just because we've never experienced a difficult something like cancer. Faith comes through hearing, and hearing comes through the word of God (see Rom. 10:17). We must be faithful to speak our faith, even when our feelings don't match up. But when a something presents itself to us, it can become the fertile training soil to grow our faith. As we submit our fears and our flesh to the refining fires of God's witness, he is faithful to bring us forth as gold. Rarely will we witness gold's grandeur on the front side of our somethings. Some gold only reflects its brilliance in hindsight.

Today I hold a nugget or two within my heart—the products of my willing surrender to suffering's requirement. I imagine my chemo friend might carry a few nuggets as well. We've lived the rigors of what cancer can do to the flesh. In addition, I've been blessed to witness the beauty of what cancer can do for my faith. Cancer has strengthened my previously held conviction. It doesn't matter how long God chooses to preserve my earthly life; what matters is how I choose to preserve him in the earthly life I've been given.

Live up to your convictions, friends. Preserve your faith; preserve the God of your faith, even when suffering is attached to that preservation. Summon God's strength to enable you to boldly live out your previously spoken faith. Calm your anxious fears with the truth that there is not a something that God hasn't dealt with before. He's dealt with it all, and the victory's been won. 'Tis a sweet trust to tether our refining process to a sweet Jesus. He will not fail us. Thus, I pray:

Father, you know our fears even before we display them. You see our hearts, and you see where we're headed. Seed your truth into our journeys through your Word, through friends, through music, through nature; whatever means you choose to use, plant and grow a strong faith within us. Our somethings are as nothing in comparison to your strong power. Apply your power to our lives. Let us see you for who you really are, and then, in holy fear and trembling, let us walk with confidence the road in front of us. Fall on us afresh this day, and keep us to your holy preservation with every deliberate step that we make. Amen.

Living Forward

- What previously spoken convictions have you been challenged to live up to in recent days?

- How is faith shaped by personal convictions?

- Write down two or three bold statements of faith that you can easily proclaim because of the suffering season you have experienced.

- Read the following scriptures, and record the significance of these bold faith statements. How did the authors live up to their spoken convictions?

  - Job 13:15–16
  - Mark 8:27–30
  - Luke 22:42
  - John 3:27–30

13

Just Breathe

But Martha was distracted by all the preparations that had to be made.
—Luke 10:40

I'M BARELY BREATHING today, not physically speaking but in all the other kinds of ways—emotionally, spiritually, mentally. It's just my life right now. Summer is in full swing, four kids under our roof and underfoot. I no longer pen a to-do list. That, in itself, feels like obligation. I'd just rather pretend that nothing needs doing and call it a win. Today, I want to breathe like Mary; unfortunately, my pulse registers more like a breathless Martha, desperately trying to get anyone to take notice.

I've never been one for the lure of summer. It feels too hot, too crowded, too noisy, too demanding. As I'm easing back into the routine of life after a long sabbatical of shut-down, it's been difficult to juggle the demands of my summer and make them fit neatly into my healing process. There's nothing neat about it; it's just mostly a messy toss-up into the air to see how it all lands on the pavement in front of me. The demand that sticks out—the one that lands the closest to my hands—is usually the one that receives my energy.

This morning, it was a phone call from my friend Martha. Yes, Martha is her real name. I couldn't help but laugh at the irony of her timing. It's been a very busy morning for my household, a day when the agenda was set long before dawn broke through. Part of that agenda included my having some time to write a few thoughts. After most of my morning disappeared due to miscellaneous mommy details, I really didn't have time to take the call. But realizing her need and, truthfully, realizing my own, I picked up the phone to receive her generous dose of encouragement. A quick prayer of confession was offered from my heart to the Father: *Forgive me for ever thinking my agenda is more important than a friend.*

Distractions, how quickly they've reentered my life. Six months ago, I had plenty of time for phone calls and wasn't worried about the peripheral issues that attach themselves to daily living. My distractions were limited to menu choices and to managing the side-effects of my cancer treatments. I wasn't worried about writing deadlines or paying bills or scheduling play dates for my kids. Six months ago, I gave myself permission to rest, to heal, and to live without distractions. One of the beautiful gifts I received in that season was the capacity and personal willingness to view life through the lens of a single, twenty-four-hour time frame. My thoughts and my worries rarely ventured beyond a day's parameters. I wasn't burdened by the daily commotion that normally presents itself as pressing necessity.

Today lives differently than it did back then. It didn't take long for temporal interruptions to worm their way back into my schedule. Certainly, they've been there all along, but as my health has improved, so has my willingness to treat them as urgent obligations. I long for the return of my previously held notions about the relevancy of worry. And while a diagnosis of cancer certainly produces anxiety and distractions all its own, it seems that I handled them better back then.

What's the difference between my then and my right now? The difference resides in the expectations surrounding my health. The greater my health, the greater the expectations from others (and from myself) to get back to routine—to a schedule like the one I kept prior to cancer's arrival. As the postchemo days accumulate on my calendar, so does my stress level, and I would be lying if I didn't confess to you that there's some personal anger and frustration mixed in as well. I don't want to live a life of distraction that leads to anger. I want to live with higher perspective, firmer resolve, and with some boundary lines around my life that allow me to breathe on occasion.

Martha wanted to breathe—the biblical Martha, not my personal friend. Somewhere along the way, her sister Mary learned how to breathe, how to pause from busyness in order to inhale life as it arrived. Perhaps Mary's temperament was more suited to breathing than her sister's. Perhaps her personal "somethings" sharpened her focus. Whatever the reason, Mary allowed her daily agenda to be tempered by the best over the better. Mary made a choice for personal health—heart health. She drew the boundary line between what was required of her and what was needed.

If you are familiar with the biblical story, then you know what Mary needed. Listen to Christ's response to Martha's impassioned plea for help: "Martha, Martha . . . You are worried and upset about many things, but only one thing is needed. Mary has chosen what is better, and it will not be taken away from her" (Luke 10:41–42).

Just Breathe

Today, as I read this passage with fresh intention, I am struck by Christ's final words to the sisters. They serve as a renewed witness to my heart today. Loosely paraphrased, "What is better . . . will not be taken away from her." That *better*? Mary's intentional breathing in of her Savior—in and out, out and in, one blessed breath at a time, as if her life depended on it. It's like a spiritual CPR that led not only to heart health but also to something better that would not be taken away from her.

I want to breathe better—a better that will not be taken away from me. I want the posture of a Mary heart like I possessed six months ago. I want a heart before the Father that has nowhere else to go, no pressing agenda to get through, no one else to turn to except the only God who can breathe his eternal witness into my life. Life's distractions will always be my portion, yours as well. Summers will always be hot, crowded, noisy, and full of demands (winters too). It matters not the season we're living in; what matters is making sure that we're breathing correctly in all of them.

Healthy breathing begins and ends with Jesus. Sometimes it takes a something to remind us of this truth, to give us permission to draw a few boundary lines around our time so that we can find a holy better that will never be taken away from us.

If you're having trouble breathing today, I invite you to pause from distraction, bow your heart, and simply breathe in the love of your Savior. Just breathe . . . in and out, out and in, until your lungs are filled with the beautiful breath of heaven. Thus, I pray:

Thank you, Lord, for the breathing seasons I have known, for all of the moments when I paused from my agenda to more fully take you in. You are so willing to be known, Father; forgive me for my unwillingness to take you up on your offer. Keep my distractions from becoming the one thing that will not be taken away from me. Rather, let your eternal presence be that one thing, my better thing—the best and most gracious grace ever received into my heart. Amen.

Living Forward

- When have distractions kept you from breathing in the presence of God?

- Why is it sometimes easier to pause and spend time with God when walking through sufferings?

- Make a list of some of the current distractions that are consuming your energy in this season. What are some practical ways to temper distraction in order to focus on the better thing that God has for you?

- Read about Jesus' visit to Mary and Martha's house as found in Luke 10:38–42. In what ways are you like Martha? Mary? What better thing is Christ moving you toward?

14

Wearing Your Remembrance

And Joshua set up at Gilgal the twelve stones they had taken out of the Jordan. He said to the Israelites, "In the future when your descendants ask their fathers, 'What do these stones mean?' tell them, 'Israel crossed the Jordan on dry ground.'"
—Joshua 4:20–22

TODAY I WORE Lisa's necklace—rich coral-colored beads mixed in with brushed silver ones, all anchored by the focal point, a large cross. In wearing it, I remembered Lisa. It came to me as a gift from Lisa's best friend, Martha (remember her?). Martha's call a couple of days ago was an invitation to lunch. I haven't had many lunch dates in the last year. My family and I had just moved to the area when I received my diagnosis. Before I had time to make friends, I was introduced to cancer. And as lunch companions go, cancer makes poor company. So I was thrilled to take Martha up on her offer.

I liked Martha the first time I met her. She was sitting with Lisa across from me in the chemo lounge. Lisa was the patient; Martha was her good friend. I was quick to introduce myself to them and to invite myself into their conversation. Their kinship with one another was obvious, and their laughter a generous grace to my day. After a few hours of dialogue, my chemo pump drained dry, and we parted company. I didn't know if I would see either of them in coming days, but I was exceedingly grateful for the gift of friendship extended to me during our brief meeting.

Our paths did cross again a few weeks later, during another chemotherapy session. The conversation picked up where we left off, strengthening our initial bonds of friendship. A chemo lounge lends itself to the birth of new friendships. Relationships made there are rarely forgotten. The intense need of the moment exposes a raw heart. Attachments quickly form because of the vulnerabilities shared.

I would see Lisa a third and final time; she was in a hospital bed, hooked up to morphine. The following day, she was scheduled for transfer to a nursing home in Pennsylvania, where her parents reside. Before she departed, I wanted to say "good-bye," a real good-bye—one spoken with the knowledge that the next time we met would be on the sacred soil of our forever home.

It's hard to know how to speak that kind of good-bye, to do it justice, and to mark it with appropriate reverence. Still, I've never shied away from the privilege of kneeling bedside with a dying friend and imparting a few words of grace and peace. Parting life benedictions are a sacred trust, a beautiful endowment to the soul standing on the edge of eternity. The earthly ground beneath our feet is never more hallowed than it is in those moments that teeter between the now and the next.

I felt it that day with Lisa, even though we barely knew each other. My heart caught in my throat several times. Choking back my tears, I watched hers freely fall down her cheeks as she smiled and reminded me, "It's OK, Elaine. I've had a good life. And I'm ready to go home."

Lisa did go home to Jesus not long after she arrived in Pennsylvania. She was forty-seven years old, leaving behind a grieving fifteen-year-old daughter and a good friend named Martha.

I didn't learn of Lisa's death until several weeks after it happened. Wanting to check up on her condition, I called Martha, only to find out that Lisa had passed away. Martha's hurt was still very raw and tender—her ache penetrating through phone lines, drawing my heart closer to hers. I promised her my prayers and asked her to keep in touch. And just today, several months removed from our last visit at the chemo lounge, we had lunch together, where she presented me with a gift, a necklace Lisa had made.

"She wanted you to have one, Elaine. She used to make these during those nights when she couldn't sleep. I thought a lot about which one to give you. I hope you like it."

Warmly moved by the gesture, I immediately wrapped the coral strand of love around my neck. Martha was wearing one as well. Over the next hour, we talked about life, about "moving on" from cancer, and about her longtime friend Lisa. Today we remembered Lisa with words and wore remembrances around our necks in honor of the woman who allowed both of us the privilege of her friendship. Without Lisa, I wouldn't have had a lunch date today. Without Lisa, I wouldn't have a Martha in my life.

Yes, today I wore her remembrance. I'll store these precious coral stones as treasures alongside my other stones of remembrance so that when my children and my friends ask me, "What do those stones around your neck mean?" I'll be able to tell them a story

Wearing Your Remembrance

about a sister-warrior named Lisa, about a friendship birthed over chemo cocktails, about how she crossed over the Jordan on dry ground to reach the Promised Land, and about how her witness brought two souls together to break bread around a lunch table.

Remembrance. What stones are you wearing today? What assortment of grateful recollection lies inside your jewelry box, around your neck, on your hand, in your heart? Are you taking time to gather stones worthy of an altar—a stringing together of commemoration that marks the faithful movement of God in your life? Are you looking for them, asking for them, anticipating them?

Each and every day, God stacks a few stones worthy of collection in the middle of our Jordans—those places in our lives that seem impassable but for his powerful, miraculous work. To retrieve them, we must be willing to make a heart's investment. Several months ago, Lisa invested a small piece of her heart into mine. Today, Martha and I took her lead and made an investment with each other. In doing so, we wore remembrance, and the ground beneath our feet shook with the reminder of home—Canaan, Lisa's new address.

Wear your remembrance, friends, and remember the God who has been faithful to stack the waters on your behalf so that you might walk through your Jordan on dry ground. Collect a few stones as you go so that in the future, when others ask of you, "What do these stones mean?" you will be able to point them toward home. Thus, I pray:

Thank you, Father, for the stones of remembrance that come to me through your powerful deliverance, for friendships, for laughter, for victories over conflict and suffering, for perseverance through trials.
Thank you for your love that heals me,
your joy that envelops me,
your peace that calms me,
your patience that teaches me,
your kindness that includes me,
your goodness that gives to me,
your faithfulness that remembers me,
your gentleness that softens me,
your self-control that makes allowances for me,
your grace that forgives me,
your light that brightens me,
your strength that protects me,
your arms that carry me,
your hand that leads me,
and your Word that feeds me.

Beyond the Scars: Daring to Live Forward

All of these are fruits of your faithfulness in my life. All are sacred stones of remembrance to be worn as treasures so that when others ask me, "What do these stones mean?" I'll be able to point them back to you. Amen.

Living Forward

- What are some of the stones of remembrance you've collected over the years to serve as reminders of God's faithfulness in your life?

- Why is remembrance important? What is gained by remembering? What is lost by forgetting?

- What are some of your roadblocks to remembering?

- Read the full account of the Israelites' crossing over the Jordan (Josh. 3–4). What key image or verse strikes you as being the heart of the story? How does it relate to your current season of struggle?

15

God Knows Who You Are

My frame was not hidden from you when I was made in the secret place. When I was woven together in the depths of the earth, your eyes saw my unformed body. All the days ordained for me were written in your book before one of them came to be.
—Psalm 139:15–16

ROUTINE VISITS TO the Wendy's drive-thru are not uncommon for our family, especially since they've added the summer sensation wild-berry iced tea to the menu. I confess, I'm hooked on it. Down south we like our iced tea; throw in a few extra berries for sweetness, and it's a slam dunk.

A few days ago, my obsession landed me back at the drive-thru. The young man working the window was happy to take my $2.12 and mark my exit with a few perfunctory words of customer service: "Thank you for stopping by our Wendy's today. Enjoy your wild-berry tea, sir."

He got it mostly right—his thanks for my patronage and his hopeful expectation for my purchase. But it's that last part that caught me off guard. The "sir" part made me pause. He didn't miss a beat. He thought he had it right, and I suppose if I were in his shoes, I might have spoken similarly. But I wasn't in his shoes; I was wearing mine—wearing a new flesh that included a flat chest and very little hair regrowth, and because I'd just finished a sweaty walk outdoors, no make-up. Yes, he thought he had it right; I knew he had it wrong. And as I pulled away with my tea in hand, I did something I haven't done for a long time.

I laughed . . . a lot. I snorted, hooted, and hollered all the way home, with intermittent shouts of, "Bless him, Lord, just bless him! He doesn't know who I am, but you do. Bless him anyway!"

Six months ago, I wouldn't have been able to laugh at his honest mistake. Six months ago, I would have crumbled into a puddle of tears at the Wendy's drive-thru because of an honest mistake. Back then, when I looked into the mirror, I didn't see beautiful transformation. Rather, I saw hideous disfiguration. I saw an impressive scar that ran the full width of my chest, smaller scars on my abdomen from my hysterectomy, an extra thirty pounds added to my frame, and a head as shiny as a billiard ball. Six months ago, mirrors served as threatening reminders to me of the reality I was living. Mostly, I just avoided them.

That was back then, and today lives a little differently for me. And while I'm still not a big fan of my raw exposure before a mirror, I've mostly made peace with the process. The weight is coming off; my hair is growing in. My scars still remain, but rather than viewing them as reminders of all that's been lost, I'm beginning to see them as the transformational threads of God's willing healing. When viewed through that lens, an honest mistake regarding my gender is simply another opportunity for me to pause and give thanks for the gift of another day. It doesn't matter if the world gets me right; what matters is that God has always gotten me right.

God knows who I am. God knows who you are as well. From the very beginning of the beginning, God sat with the idea of me and you. On the front side of Genesis, the creative pulses of Creator God included thoughts of us. Charles Spurgeon writes to this point when he says, "Before we had a being in the world we had a being in His heart."[4] Before life and breath entered into our lungs, life and breath flowed from the Creator's into ours. He was with us when we were "woven together in the depths of the earth" (Ps. 139:15).

Woven, the word *raqam* in the original Hebrew language, a verb meaning "to embroider, to weave, to do needlework."[5] Further still, it means "to variegate with colors."[6] God's palette was rich with color when we were knit together in our mothers' wombs. His palette continues to paint its witness into us as we move from infancy into adulthood. God sits as an embroiderer over our earthly tenures, needling in one colorful thread after another, until a masterpiece is revealed—a completed work of grace that will be unveiled fully in heaven.

Until then, we must entrust this work to God's heart, knowing that he isn't confused regarding who we are, where we came from, and where we're going. It doesn't matter if our bodies have betrayed us along the way, if our suffering seasons cost us a pound or two of flesh, or even if they've added a pound or thirty in return. Whatever the condition

God Knows Who You Are

of our bodies today, believing that "before we had a being in the world we had a being in His heart" will go a long way toward shaping a better perspective regarding our scars.

The effects of living in a fallen world—a sin-sickened earth—mean that our "coloring" won't always conform to the Edenic beauty imagined on our behalf by our Creator. There are other colors that work their way into our frames and that speak their witness into our masterpieces because, quite frankly, we aren't in Eden anymore. Perfection isn't our portion, and the trials that come to us sometimes weave a nasty scar into our pictures. But God's promise to us is that even the scars unworthy of Eden's beauty are scars that can be tempered by his hands. The woundings we have known, when willingly surrendered and entrusted to his care, are covered by his incomparable grace. When that happens, our scars no longer ruin the picture, they enhance it. No longer are they viewed as disfiguration but, instead, as God's holy transformation.

Perhaps you have a few scars of your own that mock you in the mirror, not only in your flesh but also in your heart—some lasting reminders of a long suffering that don't seem in a hurry to leave. Your attempts at covering them up are futile; some scars are just that bold and harsh in their witness. You want them to heal, to no longer be the source of confusion for others, but all of your attempts at masking are falling short of your goal.

I understand. Along with this last year, I've spent many years trying to make something out of my scars. Trying to make them count for something more than the pain required to receive them. They've only counted as God has made them count. And to make them count, friends, I've had to surrender their potency—their stranglehold over me—into the hands of the one Embroiderer who weaves beauty into pain, who colors grace over sin, who says, "I know who you are, Elaine, and we're getting closer to Eden's glory with every passing day."

Oh, to hold and to become that! What glory is yet to be revealed in us because of the God who is willing to weave our fallen "somethings" into his plan of perfection! We may not see it now when we look into our mirrors, but God sees it. God knows who we are and who he has created us to be. God works with the end product in mind. Even though the world doesn't always get us right, God has always gotten us right—and always will. And today we can walk in the knowledge that what is not yet seen in us has already been seen by him.

Trust in that vision, and plan on your perfection. It's closer now than it has ever been before. Thus, I pray:

Thank you, Lord, for the colors that make up my life. For all the ways you've taken my scars, my sins, and my sufferings and woven them into your portrait of grace. Forgive me when I criticize your handiwork. Weave into my understanding the truth of who I am, the person you've created me to be. I am not a mistake; there is nothing disastrous about the image I see in the mirror. I am fearfully and wonderfully made because I was fearfully and wonderfully considered on the front side of Eden. I am a creation of yours, a creative work in progress, with so many threads yet to be sewn into my story. Humbly, I yield what's left of me, Father, knowing that you will take my leftovers and make them count for the kingdom. Amen.

Living Forward

- When have you allowed the world's opinion or the mirror's opinion about who you are to define you? Why are those opinions flawed?

- Reflect on Spurgeon's words: "Before we had a being in the world we had a being in His heart." What encouragement do you receive from this truth?

- Read the following scriptures, and record how this truth is reflected in each one:
    - Psalm 139
    - Acts 17:26–28
    - Romans 8:15–17, 28–30
    - 1 Peter 2:9–10

- What personal scars remain that need reframing through the lens of Jesus Christ? Bring them to the Father in prayer this day, believing that his beauty will arise from your pain.

16

Montana Is Real

And they admitted that they were aliens and strangers on earth. People who say such things show that they are looking for a country of their own.
—Hebrews 11:13–14

EVERY NOW AND then, I hear the whispers of home. Not the home that currently houses my family of six, but my other home—my heavenly one. I suppose I've heard its murmurs more clearly in recent days. Standing on the edge of my mortality has served as a portal of sorts—a brave look into the great beyond. It doesn't frighten me as it might some people. I have long known *about* and believed *in* my residency there. No, when heaven whispers to me with reminders of what is yet to be, I am moved to a deeper place of worship with God. What marvelous mystery that he would, first, come and make his home in me and then, by his grace, invite me to come and make my home with him! It is the certain hope of my heart to be with God forever. To receive a reminder along these lines brings expectation and anticipation to my soul. October 5, 2010, would bring one of those reminders to me. It was the first day I met Sarah and the first day I was introduced to chemotherapy.

Sarah was assigned as my chemo nurse for the course of my treatment. I loved her immediately. Partly because I needed someone to love that day, someone to hold on to as I navigated my way through the unknowns of my new reality. Partly because of her genuine servant's heart that bent low to tend to my crumbling one. And partly (as I quickly discovered) because she was originally from Montana.

Beyond the Scars: Daring to Live Forward

I have a strong penchant for Montana. I nearly come undone with the mention of its existence. I've never been there, nor could I tell you much about its people. I've seen very few photographs of its vastness, and beyond Helena, I couldn't name another city contained within its borders. I just know that I love it, and it's always been my desire to go there someday. Why? Because Montana represents something to me—that one place on earth that I've decided would be a good place to grow a heart, find some rest, and sow some peace. And while I know in my mind that I can do those things here, it seems to me that it might be easier for me to do them there.

Montana is vastly different from where I currently reside. Montana has room enough for dreams, for breathing, and for wild exploration without bumping into road blocks. In Montana, the animals roam freely, and the horizon stretches endlessly from every doorstep. The noises there are God-breathed, not man-made. Here in my world, there's very little room for breathing. Road blocks present themselves at every turn, and the animals are mostly caged. I can't see the horizon for the prickly pine trees that landscape my yard, and the noises I hear silence my thoughts rather than foster them.

Or so it seems. Maybe I'm just imagining it all, or just maybe I am meant to imagine it all, to cradle the longing for another place within my heart, a piece of the country I haven't seen yet but a parcel of landscape with my name written on it. A soul craving in keeping with those of my spiritual ancestors—those who ceded their earthly citizenship to a heavenly one. Those who earnestly pressed beyond current visioning to take hold of God's truth that there was a country that belonged to them and that the one beneath their feet wasn't it. They too dreamed about "Montana"—a heavenly one. And people who dream this way, people who talk this way—people who "say such things"—give indication of an understanding that most others miss on this side of eternity.

Montana is real, and it isn't that far from here.

The thought of it unsettles me, stirs up something inside of me, and creates a hunger deep within me for something more. I want something bigger, some better way of living that, to date, remains veiled behind the realities that invade my flesh. I hunger for home, especially on days when the sweet whispers from its shores arrive on the doorstep of my heart and invite me to dream beyond my borders.

Indeed, the 5th of October was a day of invitation for me, not just to make friends with my chemo nurse and my chemotherapy, but to make friends, again, with my Montana. It was fitting that a woman named Sarah (she whose Hebrew name means "princess") would take me there. She comes from a royal land, and over the course of my treatment, she crowned my life with many reminders of home. I don't think she knew that she was doing so, but God knew. He planted her Montana within reach of mine, and together we heard it calling our names, wooing us both back to its borders.

Montana is Real

Sarah moved back to Montana not long after I finished my chemotherapy. I marvel at the timing of it all; I laugh as well, celebrating with her as she rediscovers the soil of her youth. Sarah and her husband's roots are anchored in that place. Soon she'll have a little one to tend to—to love and shape and grow beneath that big Montana sky. I don't know what she'll see when she looks up into its vastness each day, but I wouldn't be surprised if heaven were but an arm's length away, almost as if she could reach up and grab it, stake her claim, and call it her country.

People who say such things are people who know such things. And people who know such things are people who live accordingly. They aren't afraid to dream beyond their borders because they firmly believe that one day they will leave them for a better place. And because of such faith, "God is not ashamed to be called their God, for he has prepared a city for them" (Heb. 11:16).

I want to be one of them—a woman who says such things. I may never feel the earthly pulse of Sarah's Montana beneath my feet, but I certainly feel it in my heart. With every passing day, its whispers grow louder, its rhythm grows stronger, and the edge of heaven stretches closer. It's almost as if I could reach up and grab it, stake my claim, and call it my country.

Montana is real, and it isn't that far from here. Keep listening. Keep dreaming. Keep hoping, and keep watching. Home is within reach. Thus, I pray:

Make heaven a reality to us, Lord. Bring its witness to the soil beneath our feet so that we might have hope for the future dwelling you have already prepared for us. Thank you for making us dreamers, for placing an inner pulse inside of us that beats for something more. We are looking for a better country to call our own; we are longing for your holy presence that draws us home. Come and be evident in our search, Father, and keep the edge of heaven within arm's reach. Willingly, we stretch our arms toward grace this day. Amen.

Living Forward

- What is your "Montana"—the place, dream, desire in your heart that represents an inner longing for something more?

Beyond the Scars: Daring to Live Forward

- When did you last hear the whispers of home? Describe.

- What whispers of our heavenly home are spoken through the following scriptures?

  - John 14:1–5
  - 2 Peter 3:1–18
  - Revelation 22:12–21

- What part of your heavenly home are you most looking forward to? What part of your earthly home are you most looking forward to leaving behind?

17

There Is a Certain Place

Jacob left Beersheba and set out for Haran. When he reached a certain place, he stopped for the night because the sun had set. Taking one of the stones there, he put it under his head and lay down to sleep. He had a dream in which he saw a stairway resting on the earth, with its top reaching to heaven, and the angels of God were ascending and descending on it.

—Genesis 28:10–12

"I'M JUST ABOUT over myself."

Those are the words I wrote to my friend in an e-mail this morning, after she had mistakenly assumed that I would be one of the speakers at the upcoming writer's conference I'm attending. I was quick to correct the misunderstanding. I would be sitting in the audience, not on the platform.

In her response back to me, she asked how it felt to be "over myself." I chuckled while typing my reply: "The fact that I just wrote to you and mumbled some nonsense about my being over myself indicates that I still have some more work to do. Otherwise, I wouldn't have needed to let you in on that little-known fact."

Silly pride; it's foolish thinking that somehow I've fully reached a place of being over myself. There's a fine line between my need to matter and my making God matter. All too often, that line gets blurred because of the innate desire within me to make a mark on this world, to leave a trace of me that I can see in the present moment, on the front side of my exit from this earth. That's selfishness, and it is how a suffering soul can quickly make an idol out of personal pain. I don't want to use my cancer to bring attention to myself. I want to use my cancer in such a way that it brings attention to God. He's just that big of a deal. He's everything. He's hope.

Accordingly, I walk that fine line in this season of planting kingdom seeds, and I pray for a heart to know when my suffering voice is needed and when it is better kept silent. I must come to the end of myself. To arrive there, I've needed more than a lecture or a recommendation from others. I've needed a hard humbling, a strong wrestling, an exhausted spirit, and a broken heart. I've needed my cancer to lead me there. And while I do not believe that God is the source behind my cancer, I firmly believe that he has used it to get me to a place of being able to make peace with my hiddenness. I'm mostly there, but if I'm not careful to keep my heart in check, I'm capable of making more of my suffering than needs making and saying more about my trials than really needs saying.

There is a "certain place" in all of our journeys where we, like Jacob, must stop running and rest our ambitions. It is a place where rough-hewn stones serve as better bedfellows than the soft pillows that normally cradle our egos. It is a stop along the road where we willingly concede our exhaustion to a night's rest beneath the stars at Bethel, even though our fear and isolation are pressuring us to move onward to Haran. A moment when we say, "Enough is enough!" and let go of yesterday's striving in order to take hold of tomorrow's promise—God's promise, a promise authored from the portals of heaven that pledges provision, protection, and preservation.

When we are able to rest at that certain place, then we are able to rise in the morning with humbled perspective, knowing that the road ahead is paved with God's intention, not ours. It is then when the stones of our previous night's discomfort become for us stones worthy of remembrance, memorialized to the glory of God and for the advancing of his kingdom. When we've slept in God's house and climbed God's ladder with our dreaming, then we awaken in the morning no longer full of ourselves, but rather, full of our Father.

It's unlikely that many others will be around to witness the transformation. "Certain places" are lonely spaces. Your certain place is likely to be one of extreme isolation—a moment reserved just for God and you. It's better that way. Pride needs an audience to prosper. Humility needs just one—God—and you alone, making sure you are not confused about who *he* is and that you understand who you are in relation to who he is. When you stand beneath the weightiness of this revelation, then you stand closer to being over yourself.

I have been at that certain place in recent days. Cancer and all of its ramifications have brought me to my knees. It has allowed me a window into my soul, and what I discovered was a woman far too willing to keep in step with human expectations and adulation. I found a woman playing to the crowd rather than playing for the King, a woman needing to matter in the world's eyes rather than knowing that she matters in her Father's eyes. Yes, the disease that could have killed me instead became the disease that saved me from myself. God must become greater; I must become less.

And that, my friends, feels like freedom, like new life, and like joy and hope and laughter that spring forth from a deep well of understanding. Today, there is less of me than there was before, both in my flesh and in my need to eulogize my life before the grave's even been dug. Had I not arrived at this certain place—my Bethel—and laid my head upon this stone of cancer, then God's dreams for my life might never have descended from his heart into mine. I might have made it to Haran without a night's stay in Bethel, but I would have bypassed the house of the Lord, the rich presence of the Father, and the stairway that leads straight home to heaven. And to miss those three things—his house, his presence, his heaven—is to altogether miss the point of this life. God is the point of our lives; the sooner we get over the strong impressions that we have about ourselves, the sooner we live as a people who can be entrusted with the story of the kingdom.

Maybe this day you're stuck somewhere in between where you used to live and where you're heading. You're running hard and fast to get there, maybe even running away from the pain that you thought you had left behind. Pain isn't usually the leaving-behind kind. Pain is a follower, and if pain is your portion, then I invite you to that certain place of God's allowing so that you might find rest beneath his night sky. What is birthed there just might be the hope that will carry you through to morning. Come; enter into your certain place. God has something to finish in you so that he can begin his new work through you. Thus, I pray:

Thank you for that certain place in my life, Lord, that has conformed my earthly desires to more closely resemble your heavenly ones. I've been running for a while now, running from my fears and hoping they would go away once I reached Haran. But Bethel has required more of me than I imagined. My stay here has been restless and extensive, but what I have seen—what I have dreamed—has been worthy of my pause. I have seen you, Lord, and your cross that bridges earth to heaven. And now, like Jacob, I anoint this stone named cancer (insert your "something"), for even here and upon this rock, your house is being built to the glory and renown of your name. Amen.

Living Forward

- How can attention on self serve as a precursor to your making an idol out of your pain?

- How can suffering serve as a tool of refinement in regards to your "getting over yourself"?

- Describe your "certain place"—the occasion when you stopped running and rested your ambitions. If you haven't reached that certain place, what is keeping you from this place of rest?

- Read about Jacob's ambition as recorded in Genesis 27:41–28:22. What fueled Jacob's running? What fueled his resting? Which occasion afforded him greater comfort? Why?

18

Ascending to Your Overlook

When the men of Judah came to the place that overlooks the desert . . .
—2 Chronicles 20:24

I WANT TO be here today, back in the place I know as Cape Hope (aka Cape Fear Valley Medical Center). Something about its original name doesn't sit right with me—the "fear" part. Perhaps it's more of an accurate interpretation of how most folks feel when they first arrive here, but I don't see it that way; at least, not now. Initially, there was some fear attached to my heart, but today, there is mostly hope that resides within.

I've come here for a couple of reasons. First, to have my bimonthly checkup with my oncologist. Second, to do a little soul work, a little turning the tables on my suffering. This seems like the perfect overlook for reflection. Nine months ago, I first penned some words about ascending to my overlook while undergoing a second round of chemotherapy. While being given the prescribed chemo cocktail, I reflected on my experience, especially as it related to the Israelites' experience in 2 Chronicles 20.

Today, my spirit is moved again by the words of faith I wrote back then. Back then, I mostly just wrote them; today, I am living them more fully. Today, I revisit them, because God has tenderly and willingly solidified them as truth for me. Like the Israelites who faced strong armies so many years ago, I too have faced a formidable foe in this recent season. Their foes were named Moabites, Ammonites, and Meunites. My foe was and is named *cancer*. Their response to the threat that loomed large on their horizon is one that I am challenged to embrace as well. Theirs was a faith willing to be exercised; my faith is less dependable, yet willing to take their cue.

As I read their witness, even more so as I need it, I see four takeaways from their story that reflect the kind of faith I desire to possess. Perhaps you need their witness as you face your own foe—your "something" on the horizon that threatens to keep you mired in fear rather than leading you onward to hope.

First, when the enemy came knocking, the Israelites immediately took their concern to the one place, the one God, who had promised them his consideration: "If calamity comes upon us, whether the sword of judgment, or plague or famine, we will stand in your presence before this temple that bears your Name and will cry out to you in our distress, and you will hear us and save us" (2 Chron. 20:9).

Second, the corporate gathering of Israelites waited in anticipation of God's Spirit's moving; when he did, he lighted upon one of them and spoke this message of hope over them: "Listen, King Jehoshaphat and all who live in Judah and Jerusalem! This is what the LORD says to you: 'Do not be afraid or discouraged because of this vast army. For the battle is not yours, but God's. Tomorrow march down against them . . . Take up your positions; stand firm and see the deliverance the LORD will give you, O Judah and Jerusalem. Do not be afraid; do not be discouraged. Go out to face them tomorrow, and the LORD will be with you'" (vv. 15, 17).

Third, the Israelites received the message as their own, and when their tomorrow came, they obeyed God's directives, worshipping as they went. Note that in the midst of their praises, and unbeknownst to them, God moved on their behalf: "Early in the morning they left for the Desert of Tekoa . . . . As they began to sing and praise, the LORD set ambushes against the men of Ammon and Moab and Mount Seir who were invading Judah, and they were defeated" (vv. 20, 22).

Last, God's people took up their positions at the overlook and witnessed God's faithfulness in manifold measure: "When the men of Judah came to the place that overlooks the desert and looked toward the vast army, they saw only dead bodies lying on the ground; no one had escaped" (v. 24).

These are the makings of a good turnaround, don't you think? When the threat loomed large on their horizon, they prayed, they listened, they obeyed, and they ascended to the overlook and witnessed the deliverance of their God.

In the midst of all this, God was working to procure an ending in keeping with his holiness. Their obedience plus God's faithfulness serve as an example to us of corporate spiritual victory at its best. The responses from both ends of the equation—God's and theirs—worked together to solidify and set in concrete a heart truth to surpass head truth that exponentially increased as they courageously allowed it their feet and their faith. It is a truth that makes its way from the pages of an ancient story to stand as a witness for us as we endeavor to hold holy truth as our own. Theirs is a faith that I want to live—a praying, listening, worshipping, obeying, ascending-to-the-overlook kind of faith where I witness, firsthand, the deliverance of the Lord.

Accordingly, I came a little early to Cape Hope today to see if maybe God has something else to show me from this higher angle. I sit at a table just on the other side of the glass doors that serve as a threshold for certain suffering; they also serve as a threshold for certain healing. I've been on both sides of that door frame, many days with one foot in each camp. But today, I'm standing somewhere different. Today, I'm standing at my overlook. As I glance over the edge, I see no threatening enemy, just the faces of many patients who only have begun the ascent and who have yet to realize an overlook awaits them. I want them to stand where I am standing, but I'm wise enough to know they can't get here without crossing beneath that threshold.

So I say a prayer on their behalf, speak a few words of kindness as I'm allowed, and above all else, hold out hope to them. Nine months ago, I didn't see my deliverance as clearly as I see it now. Nine months ago, the overlook seemed like it would be a long time coming. But now that I'm here, the view is breathtaking, and it is my joy and great privilege to pass that vision on to others.

Today, I am turning the tables on my suffering again. Cape Hope seems like the highest, best overlook from which to make such an exchange. What beauty, what joy, what grace, what healing I have known because of my crossing beneath its threshold! It's been a worthy ascent, and I am grateful for the steps required to get me to this place of consecrated understanding.

Keep praying, friends. Keep listening. Keep worshipping. Keep obeying, and keep climbing. One day soon, you will stand at your overlook to witness your deliverance. Cape Fear will be no more. Cape Hope will be your home. Thus, I pray:

Bring us to the overlook of our deliverance, Father. We can't always find hope in the midst of our fears. Our enemy is real, and our faith is weak. Strengthen our feeble flesh for the ascent, and help us to hear your directives as we move out in faith. Keep us praying, listening, worshipping, and obeying until our feet land at the overlook and we witness the powerful fruition of your promise to us. Thank you for each occasion when our suffering turns toward your kingdom purposes. Even so, keep turning me, Lord. Amen.

Living Forward

- What place in your journey represents your overlook—the edge from which you view the faithfulness of God working on your behalf to bring about victory?

- Praying, listening, worshipping, obeying, climbing—as you consider these steps of the Israelites, where do you see your faith is falling short? What is keeping you from fully ascending to the overlook of God's deliverance?

- What are some practical ways you can begin to turn the tables on your suffering?

- Read 2 Chronicles 20:1–30. What was Jehoshaphat's initial response to the enemy's threat (v. 3)? What is significant about Jehoshaphat's petition to the Lord? What was the outcome of the Israelites' faithful ascent to the overlook? In what ways did God honor their obedience?

19

Living Your Greater Thing

"He will do even greater things than these."

—John 14:12

THE FIRST TIME I saw her, I was on my way out of Cape Hope. I had just finished my final round of chemotherapy, and she was awaiting her blood draw outside the phlebotomist's door. My arms were filled with flowers and balloons; my heart was filled with relief. As I was saying my good-byes, she was trying hard to say "hello." I recognized the social worker sitting next to her; even more so, I recognized her tears. Some tears tell a story all their own. Hers told me she was scared, that she had just received, perhaps, the worst news of her life: cancer.

I halted my steps, knelt down to her pain, and tenderly touched her knees. It hardly seemed fair—my leaving this place, her taking my place. I spoke some brief words of blessing and encouragement to her, handed her my business card, and soberly exited the building. I would hear from her several times over the next few months, even sharing a lunch date on occasion. And just today, I saw her again—six months removed from our initial meeting. She walked through the double doors at Cape Hope, where I was sitting at a table, journaling a few thoughts prior to my doctor's appointment.

I called her name, and for the next twenty minutes, we caught up on each other's ills, aches, joys, and victories over these past months. In doing so, she helped me unpack a truth that I've been ruminating over for a while now—a spoken word from Jesus, a promise that doesn't compute with my internal spiritual compass. It is one that has always confused me, challenged me, and asked me to consider just exactly what he meant by saying it. Perhaps it's brought you reason for pause in your personal exploration with God: "'I tell you the truth, anyone who has faith in me will do what I have been doing. He will do even greater things than these because I am going to the Father. And I will do whatever you ask in my name, so that the Son may bring glory to the Father'" (John 14:12–13).

Doing what Jesus did, even greater things. This feels treacherous typing it, much less laying claim to it as a part of my personal identity. Surely he didn't mean it as it sounds. Surely he isn't saying what it seems he is saying—that you and I, sinners saved solely by the grace of the cross, could walk in his similar shoes, dispensing a similar grace on similar occasions, with similar results.

Surely not. Such a gift feels too weighty. Too much sacred privilege given to human flesh. Too much trust. Too much kindness. Too much royalty. Too much inheritance. Too much glory for any one person to handle with any measure of godly humility. Too big a theology for a pint-sized, chemo-affected brain like mine to absorb.

Chemo has taken its toll on my body; consequently, my thinking isn't always as clear as I'd like it to be. So when I read a weighty statement from Scripture like this one from John's gospel, I'm easily stuck. I don't know what to do with it. How do I take what Christ says, apply it to my heart, and then live it out most courageously before his watchful gaze, in hopes that I do him some justice, bring him some glory? What could I do in this season of my life that would even come close to matching this sentiment of his heart? How can I, sick as I have been, stand where I am as a representative of the I Am and do even greater things?

It doesn't compute, but then again, neither does grace. And today, after visiting with my friend and remembering our journey together, I had a thought regarding my *greater thing*. It crept in without notice, transferring me from the lobby of Cape Hope to a night some two thousand years ago that was steeped in chaos, waves, and despair. In happened during a fourth watch, where disciples, not unlike me, took to the waters in hopes of reaching the other side without incident. It was a night when fear roared its opposition in the face of truth and shook faith to its core, a night when those who were closest to the Master needed the witness of his eternal hold. They had a night scare that required a night God and the witness of a night Word that would carry them through to the morning's light: "Take courage! It is I. Don't be afraid" (Matt. 14:27).

And with those eight words, I become less stuck in my previous ruminations. With Christ's mandate, I begin in my understanding of what he might have meant to be my greater thing. Perhaps my night walk through cancer has been, at least partly, on behalf of others who are frightened to walk a similar stride. Perhaps God in his infinite mercy and willing cooperation endowed me with the gift of his Spirit so I could cross waves and cut through currents to become heaven's extension of grace, a sacred bridge that is linking the dying, fear-filled soul to the living, faithful God.

To think that I—a single pilgrim who has known the power of an interceding Jesus to help me withstand the fear of my own night's storm—might be able to extend the courage of Christ to others in need! That, readers, is a *greater thing*, a greater work. How great to be one extension amid millions of other faith-filled extensions who are well supplied and well equipped to dispense the King's courage, not because of anything we have done but because of everything he has done. He chose to make us a part of his rich inheritance. We stand alongside Christ as co-heirs to an undeserved kingdom. On paper and in our minds, such grace will never compute. We'll never be able to make sense of the greater things he has in mind for us to do. But every now and again, whenever we pause to kneel to the needs of others, we catch a glimpse of perfect understanding. We find our place, our sacred responsibility, and our reason for moving forward with our faith in this world.

We are here for God's greater thing. I don't know what that will look like for you in the season ahead, but I do know where the fearful live in my little corner of the world. They cloister together less than a mile from my front door, in chairs hooked up to the deathblows and life-giving process named *chemotherapy*. Many are stuck in the fourth watch. Many have yet to know that God is the Master of the fourth watch, that his courage and his hands are available to them, and that just maybe those hands might come to them through a weakened vessel named Faith Elaine—hands wrinkled by years, hands weathered by understanding, hands extended in love, hands speaking the gospel truth, "Take courage; It is I. Don't be afraid."

A greater thing indeed! What a marvelous, treasured gift with which to be entrusted! I'm living God's greater thing. I challenge you to live it as well.

Never underestimate your worthiness in the kingdom of God. He has called each of us to a greater understanding of the greater gift we've been allowed. Use it all, do it all, love them all with God's greater end in mind. Thus, I pray:

Show me, Lord, the greater thing that needs my witness this week. Extend your courage and your Spirit through me. Let me not be afraid of such a weighty privilege. Instead, empower me with your strength, your love, and your mercy so that others might be able to bridge the gap between their pain and your healing grace. Amen.

Living Forward

- Consider Christ's words to his disciples in John 14:12–13. What are your thoughts regarding the "greater things" Jesus speaks about in these verses? What practical application can be applied to your life?

- Describe a time when God has used you as "a sacred bridge that is linking the dying, fear-filled soul" to himself. Why might this be considered a *greater thing* in God's eyes?

- Describe a time when someone served as the sacred bridge between your doubt and fear and God's healing hope.

- Read John 14:15–30; 16:5–16. What promises does Christ give to us that enable us to live our greater things?

20

Grieving Your Losses

"I tell you the truth, you will weep and mourn while the world rejoices. You will grieve, but your grief will turn to joy . . . . Now is your time of grief, but I will see you again and you will rejoice, and no one will take away your joy."
—John 16:20, 22

WITH EVERY CANCER comes loss—loss of health, loss of flesh, loss of routine, loss of finances, loss of connectedness with the outside world, loss of loved ones. Cancer is a costly disease, a taker. For all of the ways that cancer has given back to me, I cannot underestimate the losses that have come to me as well. It wouldn't be fair to my story. I daresay that without tremendous loss, there wouldn't be much of a story to tell, at least, not this one. But to get to the point of being able to write my story—the giving-back part of my story—I've had to grieve my losses.

This hasn't been easy to do, especially when the world kept telling me to "get on with it." Maybe it wasn't the world; maybe it was me. Either way, there really was no getting on with it until my wounded soul had time to work through the loss. I'm still working through it. I imagine you are as well. We must grieve our losses prior to our healings, and we must allow other hurting souls time and space enough to do the same.

This truth hit home for me the week that my husband I watched the HBO miniseries *The Pacific*. It was grizzly, gruesome, and full of a grittiness that exacted a toll on my senses. Still, the story was compelling enough to keep me engaged. For several nights, we hunkered down with the men of the First Marine Division at Guadalcanal, Peleliu, and Iwo Jima and watched their stories unfold.

There's so much I could tell you about the movie, so many moments when I felt as if I were there, tasting the torment and feeling the pulse of the marines who bravely manned their stations and, even more so, who heroically pushed forward when the orders were given. Their courage and relentless drive for victory are noteworthy, the makings of good headlines, best-selling books, ticker tape parades, and made-for-television movies. Without the bravery of countless armed forces, which undoubtedly served as a precursor to certain triumph, we'd have far fewer of these moments to chronicle with our token remembrance. Victories are important, but not all are won on the battlefield. Some of them are won in lesser places—the silent fields that surround a heart once the swords have found their scabbards and the guns their holsters.

Some victories arrive after the obvious. Some emerge on the heels of a battle quietly fought on the front lines of a return home—a safe landing at a crossroads in a cornfield, where the only ammunition in sight is the manure-laden field begging a healthy harvest in due season. This is the sentiment from *The Pacific* that captured my heart on the final evening we watched it—the coming-home sentiment and all that must have meant for the marines who made it home and who were willing to do the hard thing of living beyond the Pacific.

Scene after scene, I witnessed the dropping off of these men and women, back into the normalcy of what used to be. Some were returning to fanfare. Some were returning to anonymity. All were returning with renewed perspective about their lives and the questions that came alongside to challenge their former, safe parameters and sterile thinking. All of them wanted life as usual. Most of them realized that life as usual could never be again. Instead, scalded memories and harsh woundings that refused amputation from their thinking infiltrated life as usual. Thus, a new battle for home turf began within each marine's soul, with little or no support from a country that proudly displayed its flag, bought its war bonds, and wrote its memoirs.

We left them alone to fight those unseen battles and to deal with their silent pains, while bravely and arrogantly shouting, "Get on with it. Suck it up. Deal with it. Man up. That's life. Move on, or get left behind."

These are words easily spoken, words harder to receive. All were quick fixes to the problem of pain; they were boorish and rude interruptions to the process of healing. Words were often spoken when silence gripped a conversation, when answers weren't so obvious, and when the comforter was uncomfortable with suffering's significance. Instead of lending grace and time and community to a returning marine, many quickly wrapped up their comforting with cards and calls and casseroles and deemed them enough for the healing.

It wasn't enough back then; it isn't enough right now.

Grieving Your Losses

And if you think I'm talking solely about the honorable men and women who serve in our armed forces, you've missed the bigger picture, for every last one of us has stood on the battlefield at one time or another in our lives. We've all fought hard for victories that bloodied and bruised us along the way. We all boast the scars of the sacred ground we've fought to preserve—the hallowed hill we've climbed to take. And when the battle is through, when the victory seemingly is won, we, like the marines of *The Pacific*, get dropped off in our cornfields, left at our train stations, and commissioned with the responsibility of getting on with it.

A huge gap resides somewhere in between the dropping off and the getting on with it, rows and rows of planted seed requiring time and tending before moving forward with the harvest. To quickly step over those rows shortchanges the trajectory that will safely and most healthily land us at the threshold of the next chapter in our lives. I clearly saw this in the hearts and minds of those returning soldiers in *The Pacific*. I've clearly seen this in me as well, and even in some of you.

And so, today, I give myself permission to grieve my losses. I ask you to do the same. Having recently jumped off the train from battle, I willingly stand on the edge of my cornfield and wait. I see the tender shoots before me and will pause long enough to watch them grow in season, not according to the world's almanac. I will not let others rush me to the other side. They mean well with their cards and casseroles, and the best part of these offerings is nourishment for my walk-through. I am grateful for them, but they are not enough to heal me. A suffering season that has required a pound or two of my flesh, as well as a pound or two of struggling faith, requires more than human memorial.

It requires eternal mending—sacred renovation and restoration from the only one who knows what it means to suffer perfectly through to victory. God is the trajectory who will safely take us to the threshold of our next chapters. Accordingly, he meets us in our train stations, and he tells us not to rush the journey home. He says that he has time enough to linger with us in our grief. He reminds us that we are the reason for the battle he waged—for the sacred ground *he* fought to preserve, the hallowed hill *he* climbed to take. All that is required for our getting on with it is a willingness to place our wearied hands in his nail-scarred ones and to rest our wounded flesh next to his. Together, we will unhurriedly watch the harvest come in.

Victories are important, friends, but not all of them are won on the battlefield. Some of them are won next to Jesus, in the silent fields that surround a heart and life upon the return home. This is where I'm standing today. Perhaps you stand there as well. Others may see the battle as over, but I see it as ongoing, not because I have some martyring need to linger in the pain, but rather because I know that Band-Aids are poor company when wounds fester with lingering infection. Thus, I give myself permission to tenderly grieve my losses. I give you permission as well.

Don't rush your getting on with it. Simply live the grace that is given to you today. In time and because of Christ's willingness to suffer your losses alongside of you, your joy will return, and no one will ever be able to take it away from you. Thus, I pray:

In this season of returning home, Lord, I ask you to meet me at the station. To take my hand, and to lead me through to my healing. Salve my scars with the truth of your joy. Heal my memories with the truth of your cross. Repair my emotions with the truth of your love, and restore my faith with the truth of your forever. In time, Lord, when the grieving is done, use my past to further the work of your kingdom. Until then, hold me next to your heart. Only you can bring joy from this sorrow. Amen.

Living Forward

❧ What are some of the reasons behind our being uncomfortable with the pace of the grieving process? Why are we inclined to rush through it, perhaps even bury it?

❧ When have you felt rushed to get on with life, not having the necessary time to work through the corresponding grief that has surfaced because of your suffering?

❧ Take time to name your losses. Think broadly to include losses beyond the seen and measurable ones. What has your suffering season taken from you?

❧ What do the following verses have to say about the healing process?

- Ecclesiastes 3:11
- Jeremiah 31:3–5, 13–14
- Isaiah 62:1–4, 11–12
- 1 Peter 5:10

Affording Them Grace

As the men were leaving Jesus, Peter said to him, "Master, it is good for us to be here. Let us put up three shelters—one for you, one for Moses and one for Elijah." (He did not know what he was saying.)
—Luke 9:33

PEOPLE MEAN WELL; sometimes, however, they don't speak very well—especially when it comes to the suffering of others. Their words come from a place of discomfort. They are wanting to be helpful but not really wanting to stand too closely to the pain. They love us, want the best for us, but sometimes their loving and wanting isn't enough to procure a hopeful response to our pain. Like the well-meaning soul who cornered me at church the Sunday following my last chemo treatment and said, "Sure am glad that's over, Elaine. Sure am glad we'll have you around a little while longer."

What I wanted to do in that moment was grab him by the necktie, drag him to the altar, and tell him to repent for his carelessly spoken words. What I did, instead, was simply offer him my, "Me too. Me too." It wasn't the time to educate him as to why I found his words offensive. To be fair, he didn't find them offensive. He found them as a way of connecting with me. But as a cancer survivor, having just gone through the worst suffering season of my life, words like *over* and *a little while longer* didn't compute with my experience. Nothing was over . . . not yet. And "having me around" a little while longer felt more like hopeless prediction rather than hopeful prescription.

But he did not know what he was saying. Not really, and so he got a pass—a nod from my hurting heart. I was willing to afford him some grace, even as I have needed some

Beyond the Scars: Daring to Live Forward

from time to time. I've not always spoken well as it pertains to others' pain. Too often, I've said too much too quickly to do much good. Rather than taking the time to sit with the realities of a suffering friend, I've often shoved my thoughts into the path of pain's intrusion when all that was really needed from me were fewer words and more hugs—less trite and more tears. Yes, I've been guilty of saying the wrong thing at the wrong time. Thank God for his unceasing grace that never gets it wrong. Grace always gets it right.

The apostle Peter often struggled with his verbal responses. It seems as if he hosted a few showcase moments along these lines, often speaking his thoughts without giving much consideration to the consequences. His talking sprang from his passion. Peter fervently spoke because his words were tethered to strong emotion. Whether on the Mount of Transfiguration, in the garden of Gethsemane, or in a boat on the Sea of Galilee, whenever Peter spoke, he spoke the feelings of his heart. On several of those occasions, Jesus afforded him grace and gave him a pass. Why? Because Jesus knew something that most of us will never fully understand. Jesus knew just how much we would need the cross in order to make sense of our lives. Jesus afforded grace to Peter, even before Peter really understood that he needed some.

Prior to Christ's descending to earth as a baby, he saw our desperation—how very far away we were from where he meant for us to live. He saw the unspoken words of our mouths, the undone deeds of our hands, and the unfinished business of our perfection. His mission was clear from the beginning, his will fortified with the strength of all of heaven, and his earthen flesh filled to overflowing with enough grace to walk him to a cross so that we might walk there as well. Jesus understood what Calvary would mean for us, what it would do for us, and how it would shape us and create in us a willingness to afford grace to others. God poured out his grace over us and into us so that we might extend it to others. To stop short of mercy is to stop short of understanding.

And so, on the front side of the cross, Jesus afforded Peter some grace. On the back side of the cross, we've been afforded the same. God's generous dispensation to us requires our similar response to others, even when the words of their mouths don't match up with the needs of our hearts. The earth is filled with well-meaning, poorly speaking saints who are just trying to ease our suffering with a few mismatched words, just hoping to connect with us and let us know our pain has meant something to them. Just maybe, even like Peter, they are wanting to build a shelter in our honor because, in their thinking, having us a neighbor on God's mountain has been a really good experience for them. This is what I'm choosing to believe—that I matter to them and that they, in turn, want to matter to me. How can I refuse grace when such love is the motivation behind carelessly spoken words?

Affording Them Grace

Perhaps this day you know some wounding from someone's words. Maybe it was something as innocent as a few poorly chosen responses to your pain. Maybe it was something far more offensive. As survivors, whether from cancer or from another suffering "something," we live as a people with greater understanding about humanity. Our flesh has told on us time and again, keeping us in touch with the fragile human condition. We see the world through a new set of lenses, because we have been allowed a look inward at our own frailties. Thus, more is required of us, because we have seen just how ugly it all can be. The only response to that kind of ugly is the grace of the cross, both for us and for others.

I don't imagine this will be the last time I endure the honest, misspoken words of others. I suppose the same could be said of me and my mouth. But when it happens, I pray that God's good reminder of his amazing grace washes over me so I might bathe the world back with a full measure of what I've been given. I want to afford grace because of the grace I have known—yet another fresh perspective cancer has given back to me. It's not that I didn't know this before my cancer; it's just that I didn't know it to the depth I know it now. Grace is the best gift we can offer this world. In doing so, we offer them the key to the kingdom. Thus, I pray:

Thank you, Father, for seeing my need before I did, for sending grace through your Son and for making sure that it was written down in your holy Word so that I might experience it as my own. Forgive me for hoarding your grace, for the times when I've kept it to myself because offering it seemed too generous, too much mercy for an undeserving soul. I've been that undeserving soul; I've seen the ugliness buried deep inside of me. Still and yet, you afford me your grace, and you call me your own. Keep my heart pure before you as I speak my words aloud. May the generous work of the cross be afforded in them all. Amen.

Living Forward

- When have you been the recipient of poorly spoken encouragement? What was your response?

Beyond the Scars: Daring to Live Forward

ଊ Why is it sometimes difficult to speak the right words of comfort to those who are suffering?

ଊ Describe a time when someone has spoken well to you. What words mean the most to you when you are facing a difficult trial?

ଊ What do the following scriptures teach us about our words?

- Psalm 19:14
- Proverbs 16:21–24
- Colossians 3:15–17
- James 3:1–12

22

Hope Grows

Hope deferred makes the heart sick, but a longing fulfilled is a tree of life.
—Proverbs 13:12

HIS MEMORY CAUGHT me off guard, mostly because I had forgotten what he had remembered.

"Mom, we are sitting in the same place where we sat that night you told us you had cancer. It's kind of like we're remembering, like we're celebrating something."

Like a bullet, his words shot through to my heart, and I began to weep—right then, right there, in the Arby's dining area. I hadn't remembered the memory. I don't suppose that in the course of my last ten months there has been an occasion for all of us to gather in this same spot, at this same table. A table that, oddly enough, sits right beside a growing tree.

Ten months ago, I didn't notice that tree. If I did, its beauty was certainly lost on me. Ten months ago, I was choking through my what-ifs as I sat and watched my children eat their roast beef sandwiches, wondering how their hearts and minds were handling this new reality—their mommy having cancer. Earlier that day, while driving the two hours home from the doctor's office, my husband and I had stopped off at both of our older sons' college campuses to deliver the news. It had been a long, exhausting day of painful disclosure, troubling and surreal. And yet, sitting there that evening with my youngest two children in Arby's seemed like a very normal thing for us to do together—doing cancer; doing Arby's.

Beyond the Scars: Daring to Live Forward

And tonight I wonder about how we survived it—this living of cancer in the midst of normal, everyday life. Our sons had just returned to college; our youngest two children had enrolled at a new school. My husband was the new pastor of a church in a new town, with new burdens to shoulder. We had a new home to unpack, new neighborhoods to navigate, and new friends to make. There were new bank accounts, new grocery stores, a new dentist, and new routines to adjust to. So much anticipation was in our hearts for the newness unfolding before us.

There were so many unknowns as well.

In the midst of our "new" came a new diagnosis that had probably been growing in an older season . . . my last season. And I had no idea. Thank God for the previously appointed mammogram that was penciled in the calendar long before we relocated. After our arrival at our new address, I thought many times about canceling it. An hour's return trip to an old town wasn't on my agenda. But rather than going through the hassle of finding a radiologist, I made the trek back for my annual scan. The rest of the story? Well, I think you know. From that moment forward, there began an unraveling of events that has forever altered the course of my life and the life of my family.

I suppose as cancer goes, we've all managed it fairly well. It hasn't always been easy for me to chart my family's progress along the way. Cancer can be a self-absorbing, self-focusing disease at times, crowding out the needs of others. It's only now that I'm able to unpack it a bit further. What was once new to me—the new place where I'm living and the new diagnosis I am defeating—now seems less fresh, less original, more like an old season.

And just tonight, while sitting around the table with my family at Arby's, within arm's reach of a living tree, I am reminded of a very important insight that cancer has afforded me, given back to me as a treasured token of remembrance: hope grows.

Hope didn't stop in its witness just because we received some bad news. Hope kept growing, ten months' worth of growing—gathering leaves, extending its branches, strengthening its foundation, and staying alive so that my family, who once sat beside this tree discussing death, might be able to return to its shade to celebrate the gift of life—my life together with theirs. Regardless of what was going on around it, hope flourished within the life of this tree, and the metaphor provided for my own soul isn't lost on me this go-around. I will long remember this night around this table where hope grows.

Hope deferred (hope lost, postponed, buried beneath the weightiness of suffering) does, indeed, make the heart sick. But longing fulfilled (when our new becomes normal and suffering feels lighter) is, most assuredly, a tree of life. It is a moment worth celebrating, a moment to allow some tears of remembrance, and a moment to wrap up children in our arms and to say, "See this tree. Remember this tree. It's been here all along, these last ten months, and it never stopped growing, not once. It's almost as if it's been waiting for our return."

Some two thousand years ago, a similar tree was planted in the midst of suffering. Folks cloistered together within arm's reach of its witness, sharing their pain and wiping each other's tears. They thought it was the end. Their talk of death reverberated within their hearts, deferring their hope and diminishing their expectations. But three days later—a season beyond their grief—they once again gathered together to confer about the rumored possibility of new life, a resurrected life. And in the midst of their discussions, they noticed something growing in their midst. A living tree—the same tree that had earlier shadowed their grief, a branch's extension, mediating its way through a closed door and speaking some words of hope to their war-torn souls: "Peace be with you" (Luke 24:36).

Peace *was* with them. Jesus Christ stood in their midst. He showed them his season's worth of growth—nail-scarred hands and a wounded side—and reminded them that despite suffering, the tree kept growing, kept strengthening its foundation so that it might serve as an eternal extension of hope to anyone willing to sit beneath its branches.

Hope is found in Jesus. Hope is the witness of his cross and the empty tomb. How often we miss hope in the midst of our trials because of the wounding that's taking place. But if we're willing to pause long enough beneath God's tree at Calvary, then hope cycles back around to us, reminding us that he is not dead. He is alive, growing and thriving, within arm's reach.

Would you be willing to reach for hope today? To sit beneath hope's witness and to say to yourself, maybe even to someone else who is hurting, "See this tree. Remember this tree. It's been here all along, and it never stopped growing, not once. It's almost as if it's been waiting for our return."

Hope grows. Hope is here. Hope is waiting to strengthen the foundation of your heart this day. Thus, I pray:

Thank you, Father, for the living hope that authors from you and that extends its branches from the tree of heaven so that we might grab on to receive your shade and your strength. Forgive us when we don't remember your cross and all of the work that you did during that growing season so that we might forever hold on to hope during ours. You are the tree of life; keep us willing and ready to extend your branch of hope to those who have lost theirs. Amen.

Living Forward

- Why does hope sometimes get buried beneath the weightiness of personal suffering?

- Describe a time when hope extended a branch of encouragement to you during your painful season.

- How can you extend a branch of hope to someone else in a similar season of struggle?

- Read John 20:1–22. How did hope grow for the friends and family of Jesus who were grieving his loss?

23

Holding On to Your Faith

And he said: "I tell you the truth, unless you change and become like little children, you will never enter the kingdom of heaven."
—Matthew 18:3

I WATCHED HER out of the corner of my eye. Tears were forming in hers. We'd just settled into our evening routine when I noticed her sadness. The girl in me recognized her tears because I cried some similar ones in my younger years. They were tears that now, in hindsight, seem frivolous and unwarranted, yet tears at the time of their initial release that were important in keeping with the moment—a letting-go kind of moment.

My eight-year-old daughter is attached to her stuff. Whether it's her well-worn blanket, her stuffed animals, her hidden stash of Halloween candy, or her scruffy sandals from two years ago, my Amelia isn't keen on letting go of her belongings. She's a keeper of things, believing in their significance, even if they've outlived their practical usefulness. She'll fight hard for their survival, and last night would prove the same.

Occasionally, my daughter drinks from a sippy cup; she wouldn't do so in mixed company, but in the safety of our home, she prefers the cups from her toddler days. Over the years, we've thrown several out, but two remained . . . until last evening. Alas, one of the lids to the cups did a dance with the dishwasher and emerged mangled. My husband made the tragic mistake of announcing its demise and threw it in the trash can. Amelia was stunned by the revelation but was able to keep her emotions in check until the family was absorbed with the television. It was then that I noticed her tears. I asked her about them.

"Amelia, what's wrong?"

Silence. More tears. (Note to self: asking the question usually opens the floodgates to further tears.)

"Amelia, are you upset about something?"

Silence. Tears now freely flowing down her cheeks, body beginning to shake.

"Amelia, are you crying about your cup?"

Hesitantly, she spoke, carefully camouflaging her angst so as not to attract the attention of the boys in the room.

"Mommy, I need that lid."

"I thought that might be the case, daughter. Would you like to keep it in your room?"

"Yes."

"Then go get it, sweet child."

She wiped her eyes, made a beeline to the trash can and then to her room. Moments later, she settled herself back onto the couch, and all was well with her heart. I started thinking—about attachments.

I started thinking about the heart of a child who is willing to hold on to things, needs to hold on to things, even though others deem them unnecessary, unimportant, and limited in their usefulness—about what makes a thing more than a thing, about when a thing becomes valuable, and about why adults sometimes think it necessary to lessen its status.

As grown-ups, we're well informed about and well trained in letting go. We don't get too far into our maturing without experiencing a few painful releases. The capacity to let go and to do so with some measure of grace is often the mark of maturity. We preach it, teach it, write about it, and live it. My life history is replete with such benchmark moments. I hope they've aided in my development at every level, but just last night, I started wondering if maybe it's reasonable to keep some attachments to certain things, to store them away as hidden treasure because they became significant to me in a previous season. Perhaps, sometimes I rush the letting go. Perhaps you do as well.

Why are we quick to throw away the significant holdings of our affection just because they've gotten a bit mangled and torn by the daily wear and tear of handling them? Maybe, by keeping a few, we'll have a better chance of remembrance in years to come, when recall becomes paramount to moving forward. Certainly we need to mature as it pertains to our growing up on the inside, but what if our growing up is, at least in part, related to our holding on to a few things? I have no illusions that the lid to my daughter's sippy cup will ever serve as a functioning lid again. But to her, it is useful, at least for a little while longer. Why? Because it's part of her history.

Holding On to Your Faith

She and that lid have some longevity. They've shared some years together, been as close to one another as a temporal thing can get to an eternal, beating soul. When she was a toddler, she carried it with her everywhere she went. At eight, she limits her carrying to times of thirst. In another year or so, she'll probably outgrow her need for its companionship. But for now, it's still valuable to her, and I find that beautiful and poignant and a message of grace meant for my own soul this day.

She needs her lid, and I need a childlike heart willing to fight hard for a few things worth preserving, things worth holding on to because they're part of my history. Things that are meant for the treasure box and not the trash can. Things more valuable to me because of their wear and tear over the years and because of my handling them. Things that, in the eyes of others, may not seem like much, but things that are precious to me because they have "touched" my lips and made their way into my heart as a forever keeping.

I'm not into hoarding or collecting stuff for collection's sake, but I will tell you this: I'm a proponent of holding on to a few things that have become valuable to me over time. You could probably say the same. If we don't have a few tucked-away treasures from our past, then our lives run the risk of floating aimlessly through our earthly tenures. We all need an anchor in this season—a tried-and-true, reliable holding-on-to that will see us through to tomorrow. I don't know what yours is—the one thing that you are willing to dig out of the trash can and hide away as a treasure in the deep recesses of your heart—but I do know what mine is. In many ways, it resembles a well-worn, well-chewed-upon, overly used, mangled sippy-cup lid.

It's my faith.

Like my daughter and her lid, I will fight to the death to preserve that one. I will cry some tears over it and make sure that everyone in the room understands the fact that my faith isn't made for the trash can. Instead, I'll store it away where my daughter has chosen to store her lid: in my treasure chest—my heart. There is a history we share that's worth holding on to.

You and your faith share a history as well. Perhaps it's been a lengthy tenure together or a history as fresh as last week. Maybe you're just beginning to travel the road of trust with God. Regardless of the timing of faith's arrival in our lives, let us not be quick to label it as unnecessary, unreliable, or limited in its usefulness just because it's well worn and a bit mangled. Let us, instead, be quick to tuck it away as newly discovered wealth that can serve as a continual anchor for us in the seasons to come.

Hold tightly to your faith. Keep to the road of faith, good companions on the journey. Faith is the worthy preservation of our hearts. It will serve as the treasure of our tomorrows. Thus, I pray:

Make us like her, Father, a child willing to fight hard for personal treasure. Keep us from quickly discarding our faith's history; keep us, instead, holding on to its timeless worthiness so that it might serve as a certain anchor for us in seasons to come. Faith is the worthy holding of our hearts. Thank you for authoring it and for perfecting it as we continue to walk the road home to you. Amen.

Living Forward

- Take time to examine your personal treasures. What holdings of your heart serve as stabilizing anchors for you in times of testing and struggle?

- When is letting go paramount to our maturation, and why do we sometimes struggle with the process?

- When is holding on paramount to our maturation, and why do we sometimes willingly let go of things prematurely?

- How do the following scriptures validate the importance of our holding on to faith?

    - Colossians 1:21–23
    - 1 Timothy 6:11–16
    - Hebrews 11:1–2
    - 1 Peter 1:6–9

24

Speaking Your Faith

These commandments that I give you today are to be upon your hearts. Impress them on your children. Talk about them when you sit at home and when you walk along the road, when you lie down and when you get up. Tie them as symbols on your hands and bind them on your foreheads. Write them on the doorframes of your houses and on your gates.
—Deuteronomy 6:6–9

I STEPPED INTO the fray last evening. I had to. Something about the words they were shouting and the looks they were throwing at each other made the hair on this mother's neck bristle. They made my heart bristle as well. And so, I stepped in between them, knowing that, while they might be willing to throw punches at each other, they'd never do so at their mother. Over the next thirty minutes, my grown sons and I had a sit-down, tell-it-from-the-heart kind of meeting.

They sat on their beds in the small room they share as I did most of the talking. When they did speak to each other, they did so through me. It took a while for us to get past the original trigger that set their anger in motion. The deeper wounding—a lengthy history of the younger brother feeling overshadowed by the older brother—took place long before last night's harsh confrontation. It is not an unfamiliar dynamic in any family with multiple children. From the very beginning of time, sibling rivalry has been present and often serves as the catalyst to some of the worst battles waged inside the walls of our homes. It is a tenet of family living, a difficult one, yet one that must be dealt with when living in community.

Beyond the Scars: Daring to Live Forward

My sons' return home from college for the summer makes for cramped quarters in our house. When combining that reality with the heat, two younger siblings wanting their undivided attention, and no summer employment, sooner or later an explosion is sure to happen. And while other, smaller frustrations had surfaced for them in the six weeks since they'd been home, this one warranted intervention so that peace might return to our home—not peace for peace's sake, but peace for their hearts' sake, peace for faith's sake. As I sat on the edge of their anger, I spoke a few words of truth over them, spoke some faith, and asked them to consider their hearts.

"Boys, taking into account all that our family has been through this past year, you owe it to us to measure your words more carefully. When you say things like, 'You make me sick,' 'I can't stand you,' or 'I can't wait to leave this house,' well, those are hurtful words. Not just toward each other but toward your mother as well. If I've learned anything in the last year because of my standing on the edge of my mortality, it's this: the words that we give to one another matter. I don't have many more mothering lessons to give you, because soon enough, you'll be resting your heads beneath another roof. We are not promised another day beyond this one. But this I promise you; if today were to be your last one on this earth, the angry words that you've just released into the air are not the ones you'll want to leave as your final benediction. Words mean something, even when you don't think they do. You must understand that with every word from your heart, you plant a seed, either for good or for evil. And now that you are men, trying hard to live before Christ as his, you must put away your childish thinking. You must live higher. You must consider your words and measure them more carefully."

Tears poured from my eyes as I spoke my piece. When I was done, I reached over and ran my fingers through my twenty-year-old son's hair. What I saw in that moment wasn't a man, but rather a five-year-old boy frightened by life, already wounded by life because of his parent's divorce. I saw a boy just wanting to fit into this family where he has so often felt left out. I hugged him closely against my scars, and then I hugged his brother. I told them that by dawn's arrival, they'd be friends again. Dawn did arrive, and they are friends again. It took some words and tears and a holy humbling to arrive there, but it was worth the effort.

Peace is always worth the effort, and when it arrives (in part) because of the mothering moments I'm allowed, I am grateful for the privilege of sacred participation in the lives of my sons. Time is quickly passing, and life is moving forward. But for as long as they are beneath my roof and for as long as they are willing to entreat my heart, I'll be faithful to speak my faith to them. You must speak your faith as well.

It seems a simple thing, this sacred speaking; yet we are prone to our listless and stammering tongues, to our forgetting and to our postponing, to our saving it for another

Speaking Your Faith

day, until we are better prepared, freshly polished, and closer to our perfection. We wait for the appropriate time without realizing that the time is now.

Whenever heart health is the issue, the speaking of our faith becomes sacred mandate—to our kids, to our friends, to the body of Christ, and to those beyond. Whatever stage boasts our presence, our words arrive with us. And if silence is our portion, then the faith of the next generation is at risk. We should never assume our actions are enough. Faith does indeed come through hearing and hearing through the word of God (see Rom. 10:17). No wonder God strongly directs his people to impress their faith upon their children—to talk about it when they sit at home and when they walk along the road, when they lie down and when they arise. He knew that we would be prone to neglect. A faith not spoken is a faith quickly forgotten. And with our forgetting comes one of the most unnecessary and tragic ends I believe to be recorded in all of Scripture: "Moreover, in those days I saw men of Judah who had married women from Ashdod, Amnon and Moab. Half of their children spoke the language of Ashdod or the language of one of the other peoples, and did not know how to speak the language of Judah" (Neh. 13:23–24).

When God's people refuse to speak their faith, the generation of children that sits beneath their influence is at risk of losing the capacity to speak their native tongue—the language of their Father. Instead, they assimilate a foreign language never intended for their hearts. When that happens, God's words are replaced by temporal translations and no longer breathe with the lasting fullness of forever. That was and still is the danger of an unspoken faith.

The world is quick to find its voice when God's people are content to keep silent. And I, for one, will not cripple my children with a language that will never speak them into the folds of heaven. No, I will give them my faith through my words, in prayerful belief that the language of my Father will become the language of their souls. Raising a generation of faith *is* possible. In fact, it's probable when done so with a voice unafraid to speak faith's convictions and with a heart unafraid to enter the fray.

And so I say to you today, as loudly as my words can type, *speak your faith to your children*—even if they are grown and scattered and seemingly past the point of receiving your words. Embrace the sound of your voice, and let your words of faith fall as fresh seed upon the souls who are still learning to speak the language of our Father. It is not always easy to speak faith, but it is always good and right, and it is the mandate given to each of us as partakers in our Father's kingdom. It just may be the most worthy battle you will fight on behalf of the next generation. Thus, I pray:

Give us courage, Lord, to speak our faith. Script our tongues with the language of your holy Word, and sanctify our mouths for your intended purposes. Let not our fears keep us from speaking the truth of who you are, and let not our weak and sometimes feeble faith be a hindrance to those we teach. You have entrusted us with your faith story; keep us faithful to grow it in the generation that sleeps beneath our roofs this night. Amen.

Living Forward

- What role does your faith play in shaping the lives of those around you?

- Why is speaking your faith important to the moving forward of God's kingdom?

- Why is it sometimes easier to keep silent regarding your faith, especially if you are in the midst of great personal suffering?

- Read Deuteronomy 6:1–25. Record some of the instructions God gave the Israelites. What significance is attached to these instructions?

25

Turning the Page

> *Peter took him aside and began to rebuke him. "Never, Lord!" he said. "This shall never happen to you!" Jesus turned and said to Peter, "Get behind me, Satan! You are a stumbling block to me; you do not have in mind the things of God, but the things of man."*
>
> —Matthew 16:22–23

MY FATHER HAS always said, "The best is yet to be." For Christians, his assessment is a reliable one. With God, the best is always yet to be. We may see dimly through a glass in this season, but there is coming a day when all dimness will shatter into shards and be replaced by the inapproachable light of God's revelation of himself.

If the best is yet to be, then our yesterdays and our todays can't measure up to the fullness of what God has in store for us in his tomorrows. To get there, however, we must be willing to move forward in faith. We shouldn't stay bogged down with our history; rather, we should move our history with us as we turn the pages in our stories in anticipation of the next ones to be written.

Turning the page. The apostle Peter had a hard time turning the page in Jesus' story. What Peter wanted was for Christ's kingdom to come on earth without Christ's having to walk to Calvary. Peter deeply loved Jesus, so when talk of death and surrender entered into their daily routine of miracles and effective ministry, Peter responded with, "Never!" and Christ responded with his rebuke. The time of letting go was close at hand, and Peter wasn't fully prepared to move ahead with the story.

I am not so unlike Peter. In recent days, I've struggled with my page turning, none more so than on the day when I finished my chemotherapy. My eighth and final round of chemo served as a catalyst to one of the most difficult days I've experienced in my cancer journey, not because it demanded more of me physically than the previous seven sessions, but rather because of the milestone indicated by its arrival—an ending to this particular course of treatment for my cancer. And while other patients joyfully anticipate reaching this milestone, I feared its advent. Why? Because I wasn't ready to release the security I had experienced while receiving treatment. For me, the medication seemed like my best line of defense against a disease I could not control. In addition, I had formed many strong bonds with the staff and patients at the cancer center, ministering to their needs even as they ministered to mine. How could I let all of that go—the medicine and the ministry?

It was a confusing mess most days—my trying to hold on to this final page and my needing to turn it so I could move forward with the next chapter of my story. I was depressed, frustrated, and disoriented for a long time afterward. I wasn't thinking, *The best is yet to be*. Instead, I was stuck thinking that the best had already been. Forward thoughts about the words yet to be written into my story weren't registering with me, only the fear attached to my letting go. Fear was a crippling emotion with which to finish my chapter known as chemotherapy. When fear accompanies the finishing lines of a chapter, then fear carries over into the next one. Such has been the case with my story and maybe even yours as well.

Chapters: we all have them. They make up our life stories. They are segments and seasons of our journeys adequately chronicled, each ending halfway down a blank page, indicating to us and to the reader that another segue is about to begin. Not that what has been written up to this point doesn't spill over into the next chapter; life certainly spills over. Rather, we live with the understanding that some chapters must find their ending before a new one can begin. My chemotherapy chapter had to conclude in order for me to arrive at this point in my story, a point of beginning again and writing some new lines into a new chapter that will serve as a long-standing encouragement for others.

Over time and with God's help, I've been able to turn that page. Sometimes I think that what I'm doing here—with writing these words—may end up being one of the most important works of my life. It feels weighty and necessary, almost like breathing. Six months ago, I would have told you that my one-on-one ministry at Cape Hope was the most important work of my life and that writing a book about my cancer experience wasn't a consideration. Back then, I was stuck on the closing remarks of my chemotherapy chapter. It is only now, in this backward glance, that I'm able to celebrate faith's pull that eventually hauled me forward onto the next page of my story.

What once felt so difficult—the advent of my moving onward with my life—now feels more acceptable to me. The medicine and the ministry? Well, they've taken on different

Turning the Page

forms. Instead of receiving intravenous chemo treatments, I'm taking a daily pill. Instead of ministering in the chemo lounge, I'm ministering to others through my writing. By the time I reach this chapter's end, I pray that it, like the one entitled chemotherapy, will add meaning to my story.

Like me, many of you are standing on the threshold of unimaginable change. It could be:

- A new job.
- A physical change of address.
- A divorce.
- A marriage.
- Parenthood.
- The death of a loved one.
- Your kids leaving home for the first time.
- Caring for ailing parents.
- Caring for an ailing spouse.
- A new ministry opportunity.
- A new church.
- A new sickness.
- A new healing.
- A new relationship.
- _____.

A new chapter is about to begin, and perhaps you're having a hard time letting go of the last one. You want to embrace it—claim it, live it, and name it—but you can't, not yet. There is fear attached to your turning the page, mostly because you cannot adequately predict the flow of upcoming words. Accordingly, you're less willing to surrender the pen. You understand that with every chapter of your life comes a twist or two, a turn—an unexpected reality in the middle of daily expectations. It's those unpredictable turns that keep you stuck. Like Peter, you're afraid to let go of known realities because of what might happen, even if what might happen is couched in an eternal plan that far exceeds any plans you might have for yourself.

You have in mind the "things of man" instead of the "things of God." In your doing so, some chapters in your life have extended far beyond the appropriate word count. You have given them more ink than they deserve and consequently postponed the witness and worthiness of the next chapter in your story. Maybe today you need a little prod. I'm living proof that beginning a new chapter doesn't mean you forget the merits of the old one. You carry them with you as you go. But to stay stuck in old sufferings is to refuse the healing work of the cross. If Peter had had his way and kept Christ from the cross, all of us would still be stuck, and our life stories would end with defeat, not victory.

So I take my cues from Scripture. I turn the page of my story, expecting more of my next chapter than the blank pages in front of me. I invite you to do the same. I invite you to let go of what has been and to move forward with the next lines in your story. God has something more to add—a witness of his unimaginable grace and victory in your life. Live by that grace each day, and allow him to build on your previous chapters with his pen of eternal significance. May the chapter that you're about to finish and the one you're about to begin be filled with heavenly perspective and the perfect peace of the Lord Jesus Christ.

Trust God enough to turn the page. The best is yet to be. With God, the best is always yet to be. Embrace it; claim it. Live it; name it. Take God's Word on it, and turn the page. Thus, I pray:

Thank you, Lord, for adding words of meaning to our stories. Thank you for the chapters that make up our stories, even the ones that read with difficulty, pain, and confusion. You have graciously allowed our stories to serve as your witness to the world. Today we surrender the pen and trust you with the blank pages that are soon to be written. Make them count for the kingdom. Let no chapter be wasted. Amen.

Living Forward

- Give a title to the chapter you're currently living. What chapter title preceded this one? What new chapter title is waiting to be written?

- What are some of the reasons we stay stuck in our chapters? What are some of the reasons we rush through them?

Turning the Page

- Take time to reflect upon the Calvary chapter in Jesus' life as recorded in Matthew 16:21–28; 26:36–54. What would have been forfeited had Jesus refused to turn the page of his story?

- Consider the implications of skipping over this current chapter in your life. What might you miss in doing so? What is God revealing to you about himself and about yourself as the lines are being written?

26

Embracing Quietness

This is what the Sovereign Lord, the Holy One of Israel, says: "In repentance and rest is your salvation, in quietness and trust is your strength, but you would have none of it."
—Isaiah 30:15

I HAVE JUST returned from my morning walk—a weeping walk, a walk where I was overwhelmed, yet again, by the all-consuming love and presence of God. Such has been the case for me at so many points along the way during the last year. In quietness before the Lord, I have found my strength to keep moving forward with my faith. This has been one of God's most beautiful gifts to me in this season . . .

Quietness.

I live in a noisy world. Forget all the outside intrusions of loudness; the six people living under my roof produce enough volume to have the crickets begging for silence. I asked the Lord for at least one quiet child. Instead, he gave me the opposite—four kids willing to express their opinions on all occasions, just like their mother. Noise is never in short supply around our house. But quietness? Well, it's a rare gift. A gift that I didn't realize was missing until I unwrapped it during this recent season.

Cancer has been a lonely journey for me. Because of our moving to a new location just weeks prior to my diagnosis, I didn't have my normal support group to lean on when the news arrived. I left my lunch buddies, Bible-study gals, and walking friends back at our old address. I felt isolated from our new church family. We didn't have a history together, and I don't think they knew how to handle the sickness of their new preacher's wife.

Beyond the Scars: Daring to Live Forward

It wasn't their fault; it just was what it was—a new chapter in all of our lives. And so, I mostly moved through my cancer treatments with the willing help of just my husband and my precious mother. They protected me, nurtured me, and allowed room enough for quietness to befriend me. In their doing so, I found so much more than a companionship with quietness; I found a deeper companionship with God.

When there are few outside distractions to compete for God's attention and when a heart is willing to expose its loneliness before his throne, growing a friendship with God is not just a maybe but rather a certainty. A noisy life crowds out the voice of God. Noise masks the unveiling of our hearts before him and his before us. Just typing that word—*noise*—sounds cluttered and chaotic. But its contrast—*quiet*—types more calmly, more soothingly, and more ready to entreat the soul work that God intends to do in our hearts.

He's done a soul work in mine. He's done so through the quietness afforded to me in these last months. And because of this gift, this long period of introspective, reflective silence, I've come to value its presence in my life. I never knew that I needed it so much until it interrupted my noisy world and loudly demanded its due. I daresay this intermission of stillness before God might not have come to me had cancer not been my portion.

And so today, I hold the lesson of quietness as my own and try to appropriate it into my everyday life. It didn't take long for the noise to creep back into my world. The beginning of summer was an abrupt adjustment to my calmer days. And while I am grateful for the normalcy that is returning to our household, if I'm not careful to carve out times of quiet contemplation with God, agitation is often my response to the clamoring noise that surrounds my life. Without a daily pause to breathe in the beauty of Jesus, my other breaths aren't fueled with godly perspective and do little to improve the air quality in my home.

Accordingly, I take time to be quiet. I give myself permission to take long walks, long baths, and long closed-door sessions in my bedroom just to be still and to rest in the strengthening arms of my loving Father. The resulting joy that I experience in my heart—the weeping joy of feeling God's love for me—is a gift of holiest proportions. It is a gift I want you to embrace as well.

Like me, you may be in the middle of a lonely season, a time of isolation that you wouldn't have chosen for yourself, yet one that has chosen you. You cannot change the known realities that are going on in your world, but you can change your feelings in the midst of those realities. It's unlikely that your heart adjustment will come about while you're mired in the madness; however, it's highly probable that a change will occur as you are willing to step outside the chaos and simply be quiet before the Lord with no noises, except the loud, deafening roar of God's gift of silence. What are you willing to walk away from in order to receive that kind of endowment? What clanging cymbal or clamoring tongue is keeping you from experiencing the sweet peace of heaven?

Before cancer, I thought I knew God fairly well. Now, with a little hindsight in my rearview mirror, I realize that I could have had so much more of him all along—more of his thoughts as my own and more of his heart in me. The quietness of this season has afforded me this understanding. And for this one reason alone, I'd walk through suffering all over again . . . just to know him more . . . just to experience the love from him that I've felt in my restful pause and to realize that God's richest gift to his children on this side of eternity is the revelation of himself. What more do we need? He is enough.

In repentance and rest, we find our salvation. In quietness and trust, we collect God's strength. And unlike the Israelites of Isaiah's day, who would "have none of it," I'm taking as much of it as I can and then some. I invite you to do the same. Thus, I pray:

In quietness we come, Father, asking for the sweet communion of heaven. Direct us on how to remove the noise from our lives so that we might more readily hear from you. Thank you for quiet reflection and for bending low to speak your words of grace and love into our hearts. You are our rest. You are our salvation. You are our strength. As we are faithful to remove ourselves from our distractions, continue in your faithfulness to reveal yourself to our needy hearts. Humbly we move to a place of silence to receive from you. Amen.

Living Forward

☙ Take time to examine the noise in your life. What distractions, chaos, and loudness are competing for God's attention?

☙ Describe an occasion when quietness ushered in for you a time of rich intimacy with God.

Beyond the Scars: Daring to Live Forward

ଊ Read today's Scripture focus again. What brings about our salvation and our strength? Why do you think the Israelites would "have none of it"? How are we like them?

ଊ Read the following scriptures, and record how they support the idea of quietness in our daily walk with Jesus:

- Psalm 23
- Psalm 46:10
- Matthew 6:5–15
- Luke 22:39–44

27

Surviving Is a Collective Effort

When Jesus saw his mother there, and the disciple whom he loved standing nearby, he said to his mother, "Dear woman, here is your son," and to the disciple, "Here is your mother." From that time on, this disciple took her into his home.
—John 19:26–27

I HAD A decision to make when I arrived at Cape Hope last week for a routine exam. While waiting for my name to be called, I could either choose a seat isolated from other patients (there were plenty to choose from), or I could deliberately crowd in next to another patient with the idea of striking up a conversation. I suppose I don't have to tell you what I chose. Poor young couple, they had no idea what was about to happen—an invasion of the Elaine variety.

It didn't take me long to interrupt their thoughts with my introduction. "Hi. I'm Elaine, and I'm a breast cancer survivor. Who are you, and why are you here?"

Without hesitation, she began to tell me their story. She, a six-year cancer survivor with ongoing treatment for the disease; he, a husband-survivor and her support during this suffering trial. As she unraveled the particulars of her journey, her husband took her hand in his and smiled. Tears welled in his eyes, indicating to me that her pain had been his these last six years. The gesture was a beautiful grace, signifying the deep love shared between them. He'd been absent during some of her treatment. As a member of the armed forces, he'd been in and out of her suffering, but despite long separations, their love has conquered many obstacles. I marveled at their story of devotion and their determination to see this cancer through to the end—together, as one, as it should be.

Far too quickly, I was called back to the examination room. As I turned to leave, I knelt down beside them both and spoke these words while looking into the husband's eyes: "Make no mistake. Your wife is a cancer survivor, but you—fine husband—are a cancer survivor as well. Cancer is a collective disease, and so is survivorship. I am blessed to have heard some of your story. Keep taking good care of one another."

I'm not sure, but I think he squeezed her hand tighter in that moment, tears now freely flowing down both of their faces. And with our brief exchange, I heard an echo from home, my heavenly home. I was standing on sacred soil and was exceedingly blessed to be privy to the unbridled, unconditional, unashamed love between a husband and his wife. I could barely hold back my own tears, but I did manage to whisper a prayer in my heart. *Father, I don't know how the rest of my day is going to live, but I'll get up every day to have that kind of an encounter.*

Cancer has multiple victims, not just the ones who are carrying it in their flesh. Caregivers suffer as well, sometimes at a deeper, less obvious level. Their outlets to release pain are limited, but their pain is nonetheless very real, tender, and true. Sometimes they deserve a closer look from those who sit on the outside of the inner cancer circle. Sometimes they need our knees, our hugs, our prayers, and our compassion every bit as much as the patient does. They need to know that they are not alone as they walk this road of survivorship with their loved one. My family members are survivors as well, none more so than my husband. For every tear I've cried, he's cried two. For every prayer I've prayed, he's prayed more. What a gift of grace he has been to me in this painful trial. I imagine you could think of someone who fits this role in your own life, if not for you, then for someone you love. All who join us on our roads of suffering are survivors.

Jesus knew that we would need hands to hold, shoulders to cry on, and knees to bend on our behalf. In return, we need to offer ours as well. We see this understanding beautifully displayed at Christ's crucifixion: "'Dear woman, here is your son,' and to the disciple, 'Here is your mother.' From that time on, this disciple took her into his home" (John 19:26–27).

"From that time on . . ." a few final words from Jesus, spoken from the cross on behalf of his beloved mother and friend. From that moment forward, Mary's care and keep belonged to John. In return, Mary would invest some mothering love into the heart of John. Together, they shared in the grief and pain of the reality of the cross. Together, they would continue down the resurrection road until it led them both home to God. We don't know how this nurturing relationship played itself out in the coming seasons, but we do know that in that suffering moment, they were granted the gift of companionship. Jesus, better than most, understood that surviving their grief would require a collective effort. Thus, he gave them one another.

Surviving is a Collective Effort

Surviving sorrow and pushing past our sufferings in order to move forward with our lives is best accomplished when there is a mutual exchange of love and respect between two willing souls. Give-and-take and take-and-give are required if both participants are going to survive the pain. Sometimes the giving doesn't balance out between the patient and the caregiver. Sometimes the caregiver carries the heavier load. But there are others of us who can come alongside to lend support, ask a few questions, wipe a few tears, offer some encouragement, and acknowledge some of the pain. It's such a seemingly little thing to do—pausing to notice suffering. But for the one on the receiving end of our concern, it means a great deal. In many ways, our acknowledgment of the caregiver's survivorship validates his or her courageous decision to participate in a loved one's pain.

I don't know what my kneeling accomplished last week; it does, indeed, seem like a small thing in the grand scheme of this couple's pain. But I know what it means to me to have my suffering acknowledged, and I've watched my husband benefit from the same consideration. It means everything to us, and I don't want to go through the rest of my days skirting around the issue of human pain. I want to make a deposit into the lives of those who are hurting, within arm's reach—to be a kneeler, with holes in my jeans and dirt on my knees because of my willingness to bend and to bow and to say, "You are a survivor!" Sometimes it is the best gift we can give to one another—our knees, followed by God's words of grace.

Would you bow on behalf of someone today? Would you be willing to notice the pain of those who are suffering in the flesh and those caregivers who most closely suffer with them? Perhaps God is prompting your heart in this very moment to move into action. Don't wait until tomorrow. From this time forward, their pain belongs to you, even as your pain belongs to them. Remind them, even as you remind yourself, of your collective survivorship. It is such a small, simple grace that reaps bountifully for the kingdom of God.

Kneel now; kneel often. Kneel low, and kneel always in the strong and mighty name of our Lord Jesus Christ. You give to the King when you kneel to the needs of his children. Thus, I pray:

Thank you, God, for the fellowship of your saints. Thank you for the gift of family and friends who choose our sufferings as their own. Keep us mindful of their survivorship alongside ours. Show us how we might best support them in this time of painful trial. Let us not become so focused on our own needs that we forget the needs of those around us. Instead, teach us how to bend our knees, bow our hearts, and surrender our love to your hurting children. Amen.

Living Forward

- Who have been your primary caregivers during your time of suffering? Describe some of the special gifts you have received from them.

- How has your suffering impacted the lives of your caregivers?

- What are some practical ways you can kneel beside your caregivers to recognize their needs and to offer them support as they fight for personal survivorship in addition to yours?

- Take time to reflect on Jesus' words from the cross as found in John 19:17–27. What means the most to you about Christ's words to Mary and to John?

28

Gracing the Stage You Stand Upon

Peter turned and saw that the disciple whom Jesus loved was following them . . . . When Peter saw him, he asked, "Lord, what about him?" Jesus answered, "If I want him to remain alive until I return, what is that to you? You must follow me."

—John 21:20–22

SINCE MY DIAGNOSIS in August of 2010, I've lost four friends to cancer. Today, two of my cancer companions are in the care of hospice, and these are just the ones I know by name. When I consider the many patients who have crossed my path in this last season, I imagine that some of them have already been memorialized by family and friends at their funerals. It hardly seems fair—these varying degrees of cancer that claim a life more quickly than others. Why do some of us stand on stage I and others on stage IV?

Staging: a tool used by doctors to determine the severity of a person's cancer based on the extent of the original tumor and whether or not the cancer has spread to the rest of the body. Cancer is staged on a scale of 0–IV, with a variety of tests implemented to determine the staging of a patient. *Carcinoma in situ* receives a 0 stage because the abnormal cells haven't spread to surrounding tissue. With stage IV, the cancer is invasive and has spread to other organs in the body. Stages I, II, and III are somewhere in between these two extremes, and within each stage, are subcategories to further delineate the progression of cancer.

Beyond the Scars: Daring to Live Forward

I'm standing on stage IIB. Many of my friends were ushered onto stage IV without ever realizing there was a stage 0, I, II, or III. Why all this talk of staging? Why does it matter? And what does it have to do with laying claim to a stronger spirit?

With staging comes understanding. The diagnostic nature of the staging process allows the cancer patient a clearer picture about the road ahead. This doesn't mean that a number should be the defining factor patients use to gauge their hope for survival. That being said, I am convinced that staging does have a direct effect on our perspective as we move in and out of the treatment process. The disparity that often exists between the different stages is a wrestling within my heart some days.

I have often wondered about how differently my life might be today had I landed on stage IV instead of stage IIB. I have thought about what a few more months of waiting for that mammogram might have cost me . . . perhaps pushing me onto stage III or IV. I don't linger there very long; it's not my reality, and there is little to be gained by traveling through the land of what-ifs. But every now and again, I go there, because I have a multitude of friends who are standing there—on stage IV.

As I marvel at their fortitude, I consider my own fragility as it pertains to my assigned stage. If I were stage IV, would I be writing this book? Would bitterness be my portion? Would I willingly dig deeply for a stronger spirit, or would I be content to bury it beneath the weight of self-pity? These days I don't ask, "Why me, Lord? Why do I have cancer?" but rather, "Why stage II and not stage IV? Why are my statistics charting higher for a five-year survival than my contemporaries—those who wear the ribbon like me but who stand on a different stage? Why are some of us given seemingly less to carry and others seemingly more than a reasonable allowance?"

Staging questions are not unfamiliar territory for any of us, whether a cancer patient or not. Comparing our personal stages to the stages of others is a common, albeit usually fruitless, wrestling. The apostle Peter certainly had some staging questions regarding his future. Take time now to reread today's Scripture focus from John 21. Peter was concerned about survival statistics, not just his but John's as well. Jesus didn't allow Peter to stay stuck in his ruminations. Instead, he simply responded with, "What is that to you? You must follow me." Christ's answer to Peter's question is enough to quell the unsettled murmurings of my own ruminations. Christ's response begins with a *you* and ends with a *me*. A Jesus *me*, not a Peter *me*. "You must follow me."

And so must I follow Christ. The stage that I'm currently standing on, IIB, is the one platform I've been allowed in this season. It is a stage upon which to tell my story, a stage well stocked with scenery, lighting, props, and sound equipment to adequately frame my witness of hope. It would be easy to qualify my stage as a lesser one in comparison to those who are standing on stages III and IV. But in doing that, I would underestimate

Gracing the Stage You Stand Upon

the worthiness of those patients who are standing on stage 0 and I . . . maybe even those who aren't currently standing on the stage of cancer but on another stage of suffering.

We must not, nor should we, stage our sufferings in comparison to others' sufferings. Our "somethings" stand on a stage all their own and are significant in the eyes of the Lord. He can use them all to proffer hope in our hearts and in the hearts of a generation struggling to understand the greater things of God. We must grace the stage we stand upon instead of rushing the stage of another. The voice of hope gets muffled when too many people stand on a stage they were never meant to grace. Stage 0 stands alone. So do stages I, II, III, and IV. I cannot crowd out their witness just because I think that, if I suffer more or suffer less, I'll do more or do less for the kingdom. I can and should only do the more and less of my stage IIB. It is enough for me to stand there, and for you, it must be enough to stand on your stage as well.

There will always be disparity between the stages we're allowed. We cannot change the suffering platforms that cradle our stories. However, we can change the way we take our cues, make our marks, and speak our lines. Never will God's spotlight be more visible upon us than when we're standing exactly where we should be and are living the script authentically, without edit and without compromise. When that happens, our staging no longer matters. Hope is revealed, and God receives the renown he is due.

What stage are you standing upon this day? What allowance, what platform, what privilege rests beneath your feet? I have an inkling that it probably doesn't look exactly like my stage IIB, but its witness is just as vital. Wherever you are, whatever the stage that hosts your story, grace it with your presence. Gladden it with your spirit. Bless it with your heart. Call it *significant*, and name it as *purposeful*. Follow God's cues and no one else's. You were meant for the stage, and the curtain's been raised. Now is your time to shine. Thus, I pray:

Come, Father, and shine through us on the stages we're standing upon. Keep us from looking too closely at the stage of our neighbors—from thinking that we should be someone with more of a stage or less of a stage. Protect us from worrying about the future. Keep us focused on the crowd in front of us, and keep us honest and humble as we speak our lines. Grace our stages with the grace of your presence, and bless our hearts with the grace of your cross. Amen.

Living Forward

- What stage are you currently standing upon? Describe.

- Have you compared it with the stages of others around you? If so, how?

- Why is comparison dangerous? How might it be beneficial?

- As you stand on your stage this day, what is the one message—the one line—you'd most like to share with your audience?

- What can you learn about gracing your stage from the following scriptures?

  - Matthew 20:20–28
  - John 21:15–25
  - 1 Corinthians 12

29

Clutching Truth

We proclaim to you what we have seen and heard, so that you also may have fellowship with us. And our fellowship is with the Father and with his Son, Jesus Christ. We write this to make our joy complete.
—1 John 1:3–4

I FOUND IT this morning in the place I've been finding it most mornings since first receiving it—in my grip. It's my clutching cross—a smooth, curved piece of cedar that fits snuggly within my grip. A retired minister from our conference sent one to me after hearing of my diagnosis. He makes these crosses as a ministry to cancer patients. As a cancer survivor himself, he understands the witness of a dark night's wrestling and the critical importance of having the cross nearby to serve as a penetrating light to that darkness. My clutching cross has not become an idol to me; rather, it serves as a token of remembrance for me, for recalling the truth that I am hidden within the power of that cross—beneath it, surrounded by it, immersed in the meaning of it—despite the carnage going on around me.

I need this remembrance today just as much as I needed it a few months ago. Today, I woke up exhausted from my life. My weariness is partly the result of having subjected my body to a grueling workout over the past year. It's also part of being a mother of four. Together, treatment and mothering have added to my tiredness, and today, I'm hoping to move past it in order to accomplish something beyond just getting through it. Kingdom productiveness is what I'm after. And so, with clutching cross in hand, I begin my day with Jesus. I shut my bedroom door, shut my eyes, and whisper a quiet prayer: *Show me, Jesus, more of yourself today.*

Beyond the Scars: Daring to Live Forward

My Bible is opened to the apostle John's first letter, and I am immediately overwhelmed with his words about being an eyewitness to the Word . . . about hearing Jesus, seeing Jesus, touching Jesus, and now penning that truth into holy, forever remembrance. These words were written so that on a day like today, when I awaken to my weariness, I am reminded of a real Jesus who lived on earth in a real season and who is still making himself really evident to his people. If my tears and the warmth that I feel in my heart are indications of that realness, then I, like John, can say to you with all the authority of Scripture: "That which was from the beginning . . . this we proclaim concerning the Word of life. The life appeared; we have seen it and testify to it, and we proclaim to you the eternal life, which was with the Father and has appeared to us" (1 John 1:1, 2).

Unlike John, I haven't seen Christ hanging on a cross or touched his scars. I haven't shared a walk with Jesus on a Judean hillside or witnessed the feeding of the five thousand. I wasn't there two thousand years ago when the earth shook and the temple curtain tore in two on that first Easter morning. But I have seen Christ in my heart and felt the blood of his cross wash over my sins. Daily, I've been fed by his Word, more than five thousand times, and sensed the earth shake beneath my feet in that moment when his Easter witness came home to rest in my heart. The whispers of his voice are all around me, evident to me through his Word, his people, his world. He's just as real to me today as he was to John back then, and he's just as willing to be known.

Jesus Christ didn't stop being personal when he took his rightful place beside the Father following his ascension. Jesus Christ came to earth to pitch his tent near ours and then, through the power of his Holy Spirit, to move his tent indoors, inside the interior of our hearts. He has not left us, readers. As Christians, we can know that the kingdom of God lives within us (Luke 17:20–21). On tired days. On cancer days. On suffering days. On confusing days. On celebration days. No matter the days that come to us, our Savior lives them with us.

Without Jesus Christ, I would have no lasting witness to offer you today. I would have no bold proclamations of faith to live by, no words of certain hope, and certainly, no clutching cross to cradle in the palm of my hand. My sleepless nights would awaken to days of aimless wandering, and my getting through would be the rule rather than the exception. But having Christ in my heart doesn't mean that I'm any less tired this morning. It simply means that I can greet this day with his strength undergirding me, his hand guiding me, and his grace granting me the gift of his presence along the way and as I go. This is the truth that I proclaim to you. In doing so, I am set free from the lies that seek to keep me silent beneath the weightiness of my temporal condition.

And so I ask you, what truth are you proclaiming today? What "cross" are you clutching tightly in your grip? What word has come home to rest in your heart? What

Clutching Truth

holds you through the night and carries you through to morning? Not all our answers will procure the same conclusions. Some of you may not know or appreciate the Jesus I'm talking about. The cross in your grip may not be one of representative grace and mercy but rather of anger, bitterness, cursing, and vengeance. Your truth will be shaped by your grip and your bold proclamations therein. I cannot choose truth for you any more than I can shove my cross into your hand and force you to grip its worthiness. Those wrestlings are between God and you.

I can, however, offer you this word of encouragement. If you choose to engage with those sacred wrestlings, do so in the light and witness of God's Word. Don't make up "truth" about him; don't rely solely on the testimony of others regarding the person of Jesus Christ. Read his story, and find out for yourself. John's gospel and his letters are a good place to begin the conversation. Dig there long enough, sit there with your heart wide open enough, and you will find the answers you are looking for—the hope you're longing to hold as your own.

God's truth is the clutching kind of truth and the tenacious, willing grip of my hands and heart. I'm the willing grip of his hands and heart as well. Lovingly, he holds me close and calls me his child. Rooted there and growing there, I'm living my hope forward. I'm writing it as well. No night in my life has been so dark, so heavy, or so long that it has shrouded the witness of morning's arrival. Morning always breaks through. Light always trumps the darkness. The empty tomb always upstages the bloodied surrender, and the cross of Jesus Christ always proves true over the deceitful lies of the enemy. The cross holds me, keeps me, and reminds me of the overriding purpose of my life—to know God more fully with every passing day and then, out of that knowing, to lead others to know the same.

That which was from the beginning—Jesus Christ—still is. Take time to know God today, and cling tightly to the truth of his cross. It is the most worthy clutching of your heart. Thus, I pray:

May the words of my mouth, Father, and the meditations of my heart be found acceptable in your sight, my Strength and my Redeemer. Keep me gripping tightly to your truth, keep me digging in expectation for the mighty revelation of your witness. Forgive me when I settle for less—for the lies that camouflage as truth and proffer destruction rather than promise. In your cross, I anchor my hope and my sleep as well. Even so, breathe on me, breath of God, and carry me through this day. Amen.

Living Forward

- What "cross" are you clutching this day?

- What two or three truths have carried you through your darkest nights? Who authored those truths? What role has God played in your discovering of the truth?

- Describe a time when the witness of God's presence has been clearly evident to you in your time of suffering.

- Read the following scriptures, and record the truth you learn about Jesus Christ—God's Word to the world:

    - John 1:1–18
    - John 21:24–25
    - 1 John 1:1–10

30

Never Take More Than You Need

*Then the Lord said to Moses, "I will rain down bread from heaven for you.
The people are to go out each day and gather enough for that day.
In this way I will test them and see whether they will follow my instructions."*
—Exodus 16:4

"MY MOMMA ALWAYS taught me to never take more than I need. So keep your money, ma'am. You need it for your family. I've got enough to see me through."

Those were her words to me when I tried to give her a little money yesterday afternoon. She was pulling a suitcase down a well-trafficked road when I passed her in my van. I commented to my son about her poverty . . . about how very sad it made me to see a life reduced to a suitcase and to wandering. We didn't get very far in our travels before I turned the van around.

"Where are we going, Mom?"

"Back to her, to help her."

After turning into the parking lot where she was standing, I rolled down my window and extended some money in her direction. She was gracious, lively, and unwilling to take my offering. Her homeless status was not in question, but she was quick to assure me that she was going to be fine and that she had enough money for a day's worth of living. Mary is her name, and while our paths may never cross again on this side of eternity, the memory of her words will stay with me until then. In that moment of her releasing them to me, I felt the poverty of my own soul—thinking, perhaps, that maybe she wasn't the wandering one, the needy one. Maybe I was . . . a woman prone to taking more than what I need.

Throughout the course of my cancer journey, I've been the recipient of the gracious blessings of others. Cards, calls, gifts, food, donations, child care, prayers, and promises of help should future needs arise were abundantly present on the front end of my diagnosis. Many were the occasions when all I could muster in the way of thanks was a puddle full of grateful tears. I was overwhelmed by the sacrificial kindness of so many, stranger and friend alike. Never in my life had I experienced the bounty of such collective love. Every day I was stocking my pantry with manna from heaven, and every day it was more than enough to quell the simmering pain that fought hard to supplant goodness.

After a while, however, the giving slowed down, and I began to feel sorry for myself. The once amply stocked pantry dwindled down to sparse crumbs, and I wondered if perhaps pain and suffering have a shelf life with others. Why was it that when my diagnosis arrived, there was a ground swell of support, but when treatment was mostly finished, barely a notice from others? Just yesterday, I received a note from someone who used the phrase, "Now that your cancer is over." I've had a difficult time making peace with that statement. Cancer is never really over for the patient. It does move in and out of its severity, but the effects of having been through the rigors of treatment are long-term and require ample time for healing.

As I am cycling out of this painful season, God placed a homeless woman in my path who, unbeknownst to her, spoke a few words of teaching truth that I needed to hear: *Never take more than you need.* I have a feeling this has been a guiding principle for her throughout her life. Receiving help as she needed it but declining it when she had enough. Oh, for a heart like hers to know when to take and when to give back. When to say, "Yes," and when to say, "I have enough for today. You keep it for your family."

Our spiritual ancestors had a difficult time discerning that balance too. Manna from God was a daily dispensation and their gathering of it a daily obedience not to be taken advantage of but to be celebrated, to say back to God, "Yes, and this is enough for today." When they didn't—when stocking the pantry took priority over receiving the daily provision of God—the resulting consequences didn't allow them to profit from their hoarding: "However, some of them paid no attention to Moses; they kept part of it until morning, but it was full of maggots and began to smell. So Moses was angry with them" (Ex. 16:20).

Could it be the same for us in our hoarding of blessings? Could we, in the receiving of blessing upon blessing a few thousand times over, get to the place of keeping them for ourselves? Worse yet, could we get to a place of coming to expect them as our right rather than to humbly receive them as a grace from God? When is God's enough enough

Never Take More Than You Need

for us? Why does abundance sometimes breed greediness? Why doesn't God's daily provision settle down within our hearts as faith rather than distrust?

I think this is it. I think we are afraid that God's goodness has a limit. We falsely reason that even though today it's raining manna, tomorrow it might be raining famine. So we collect and hoard and relish our abundance; in doing so, we break ranks with God's mandate to live daily beneath his provision. We cultivate a deserving attitude because, after all, we are God's children on the road to the Promised Land. Before long, the stench of maggots has replaced the once-sweet smell of God's enough, and the odor emanates upward to the nostrils of heaven. And we wonder where it all went wrong. When did the manna turn to maggots, and why do we feel so empty on the inside?

Manna begins its disintegration when we take it upon ourselves to manage the blessings of God. Certainly, we need them, especially the witness of God's love to us through others in our times of great trial. When the need is great, the manna rains down proportionally—maybe with a generous dispensation to last us beyond the borders of a single day. But when our need is less, we must relinquish our expectations for more and live within the boundaries of a day's worth of manna. When the need is but a day's worth, the manna will fall accordingly. Out of his abundance, the Father gives to us what we require. We must receive it with thankfulness, and then we must release our expectations.

Yesterday, there wasn't a maggot in sight while I was talking to Mary, only the sweet aroma of her trust. I imagine that she has known times of both abundance and famine throughout the course of her life; yet she chooses dependence on God for his daily faithfulness. She expects neither more nor less from him, just enough—a day's worth of grace for a day's worth of living. Mary may not have needed my money, but I certainly needed her witness.

Never take more than you need.

This is a good lesson from a homeless woman and a holy mandate from our faithful God. Accordingly, keep trusting God for your daily manna. As it arrives, gather it with thankfulness, knowing that with each day's offering, God will be faithful and generous to supply you with enough grace to feed your need. Thus, I pray:

Thank you, Lord, for supplying your manna to meet our daily needs. Forgive us for thinking we deserve more. Indeed, we are a needy people, but you are our faithful God. You will supply all our needs according to your riches in glory, and those glorious riches far exceed what our minds conceive from this earthly vantage point. Bless the Marys of this world—those who are faithfully walking each day, believing in your provision. Give me a Mary heart and a Mary trust for the day that lies ahead. Amen.

Beyond the Scars: Daring to Live Forward

Living Forward

- Describe a time when you received the rich "manna" from heaven during your suffering. Was it more than you needed at the time? How did your receiving of it shape your future expectations regarding its dispensation?

- When have you felt the manna was not enough?

- Have you ever felt that your pain has a shelf life with those who walk the road with you? Describe.

- What are some of the potential dangers of taking more than you need?

- Take time to reflect on Exodus 16. What do you consider to be the most important takeaway truth from God's interaction with the Israelites?

31

Sending Flowers to the Living

But encourage one another daily, as long as it is called Today, so that none of you may be hardened by sin's deceitfulness. We have come to share in Christ if we hold firmly till the end the confidence we had at first.
—Hebrews 3:13–14

HER WORDS FELL into my heart with the force of a rushing waterfall. Hearing her voice was like a dam breaking forth onto parched land. We hadn't talked in nearly three weeks; her lengthy hospital stay was the culprit. While she and her husband were preparing their hearts for the seeming beginning of her earthly end, I was sitting a country span away from her, preparing for the same. My heart was breaking in a thousand ways because of the miles between us, even more so for the reality of cancer's grip in both of our lives. When we finally connected, we collapsed beneath the weightiness of the moment. We cried together, imparted a few words of encouragement to each other, and then released one another to a good night's sleep, she on the west coast, I on the east.

Last night, we took the time to give one another a flower—a stem or two of gracious encouragement—so that our momentary grief might be overcome by the beauty of a budding friendship. In doing so, we acknowledged the gift of life and the Giver of life, the confidence we both "had at the first" and that threads us through to today. It is a confidence that allows us to live as hope-filled survivors, keeping our hearts softened for the kingdom work that surrounds our souls. Encouragement—imparting courage to one another—is a portion of that work. When we give our words and lend our strength to one another, we add a flower to the bouquet of God's love.

"Send flowers to the living." I remember the first time those words were given to me. They were authored by the wisest woman I know, my mother, on the occasion of my preparing a speech in honor of my father's retirement from Asbury Theological Seminary. The gala event would be well attended by many of his colleagues and close friends, along with a couple of other retiring professors who also would be acknowledged. Each retiree had the privilege of choosing one family representative to speak a few words on his behalf. Feeling the pressure of having been the chosen one from our family camp, I called my mother one afternoon and asked her for some advice. I was struggling for words, for perspective, for confidence.

Her response is as clear to me today as it was ten years ago:

> Elaine, we do a really good job of sending flowers to others once they've passed away. We litter their caskets with colorful sprays, hoping that in some way they symbolize our respect, our gratefulness for the life represented therein. We wait until someone is gone before we speak our words of thankfulness regarding his or her witness. But rare are those who take the time to send flowers to others while they are still living. Elaine, send a flower to your dad on the night of his banquet. Give him your words while he is still living. That will be enough.

They were enough, and since that night so long ago, I've had many more occasions to add to my father's bouquet—to my mother's as well. Family, friends, and even strangers often receive a flower from my pocket, not because I'm the resident floral expert on handing out flowers but because I've seen the worthiness of what a single bud can do and how encouraging words burst forth like blossoms in springtime in the midst of winter's bite. I've seen the beauty of God's colors splash onto the darkened canvas of a hurting heart, and I've witnessed new life emerge in the perilous grip of death, all because of one word, one grace, spoken on behalf of the fragile heart.

Our words mean a great deal to others and to us as well. Words released as flowers are words that carry us through our seasons of deepest darkness. They brighten our spirits. They lighten our loads. They keep us from lesser feelings—lesser attitudes—that, if not guarded, could quickly morph into lesser behaviors. Anger, bitterness, selfishness, waywardness, faithlessness, fear, pity, envy, and blame, are all possible, lesser products of the heart when words of kindness and encouragement aren't extended as healing replacements.

Sending Flowers to the Living

Rarely is our neglect intentional; mostly we don't think about our words as being an investment into the heart of another. But sometimes we forsake the "giving of flowers," keeping our words to ourselves because it's hard to speak them. The emotional toll that honest words require can be exhausting, raw, and exposing, thus the reason so many important conversations never take place between two hearts. Instead, we sometimes choose our silence because the contrast is too much of an honest look into our flawed and fragile hearts. Self-preservation over personal revelation becomes the order of the day. When that happens, hearts remain as they were—unchanged, unmoved, and uncolored by the witness of a flower or two given in the name of love.

Whatever our reasons for keeping our silence, we must understand that some lives will come to an earthly close without the blessed benedictions due them. Words of blessing are reserved for a funeral, when in reality, so many of them should have been spoken in advance. Words spoken at a funeral, flowers given then? Well, they're likely to be forgotten, to decay over time, buried alongside the casket. But words of encouragement spoken into a heart before a heart moves home to heaven? Those are eternal words that never die. They blossom as a witness to generous grace and serve as a lasting memorial to the human spirit and to the God who puts eternity into the hearts of all humankind.

And so I say to you, even as my mother said to me many years ago, send flowers to the living. Take time today to say a few words and invest some encouragement into the hearts of family members, friends, and even strangers who cross your path. Let them know they matter—that they are significant, worthy, and valuable to you. As long as today is called today, extend God's encouragement to those around you. In doing so, you add a flower to the grace-filled bouquet of God's love. Thus, I pray:

Seed our hearts with the flowers of your grace, Lord, and show us when, where, and to whom we should release them. Override our stinginess with your endless willingness to invest love into the hearts of your people. Thank you for the privilege of being kingdom florists and for giving us ample vases to fill with your blooms. When words fail us, give us yours. When busyness consumes us, slow us down. When fears assail us, restore our peace. And when opportunities present themselves, grant us courage to reach into our pockets, extend a flower into the hand of a friend, and speak blessing as a living hope. May our hearts always be a reflection of yours. Amen.

Living Forward

- Describe some of the recent "flowers" given to you through others.

- Why is it sometimes difficult to send flowers to the living?

- Who needs a flower from you today? Give the flower some texture—a color, a name, and some words to describe what you need to say.

- Read John 14, and write down some of the flowers Christ gave to his disciples prior to his death. How do his words bring a strong encouragement to your heart this day?

Rethinking Time

Now he had to go through Samaria. So he came to a town in Samaria called Sychar, near the plot of ground Jacob had given to his son Joseph . . . When a Samaritan woman came to draw water, Jesus said to her, "Will you give me a drink?"

—John 4:4–5, 7

THERE'S BEEN A shift in my thinking—a major shift to a principle that I hope will stick to my heart as forever truth. I'm not sure of the day it first arrived in my thoughts as revolutionary, but I am certain of its Author. I've been thinking on it for the better part of a year now, and I plan on keeping it as a life principle rather than as a passing rumination. The shift? Well, it revolves around the one privilege that each of us clings to as a personal entitlement . . .

Our time.

Could it be that we've gotten it wrong all these years—this idea that the most precious gift we have to give to one another is our time? There's some pride attached to this concept, as if we're doing someone a favor by allowing him or her a few moments of our time. Agendas filled with, "I'll pencil you in at 3:00 P.M." or, "I'll make some time to talk to her this afternoon," keep the control in our courts, keep us thinking we're the ones making the sacrifice and that the person on the receiving end should be grateful we're going to the effort.

Time to rethink our time, readers, and here's the essence of the strong shift that's taken place in my heart. Time isn't the gift that I generously give to others. Time is the gift that others generously give to me—their time. It's all about their time and their allowing me a few moments of their day. Every phone call; every conversation; every piece of correspondence; every salesperson; every joy, tear, and disagreement shared. Every human exchange is now viewed as a gift of time given to me by someone else. No more "I'll pencil you in." Instead, "Thank you for penciling me in. Your time is precious, and you're allowing me a portion of it. What rich treasure! What surrender! How blessed am I to be given the gift of your time."

That's it . . . the huge shift that's taking place inside my heart. I think it has a lot to do with all the many hours I've sat around being a sick person in the course of a year. I've listened to a lot of stories and shared in the trauma and triumphs of a great many survivors. I've had ample time to pay attention to others; in doing so, I began to rethink my time. It wasn't about my allowing them to vent—the surrendering of my precious hours to serve as the fertile soil for their seeds of therapeutic murmurings. Instead, it became about my being allowed into the very private and personal sanctums reserved as hallowed ground for the survivor's soul. I marvel at what I've been told, the secrets that have been revealed, the hearts that have been split wide open so I could reach in and grab some of the pain for myself. It's not been about what I have given to them; it's been about the rich privilege they have extended to me. Thus, a monumental shift in my thinking has happened. I'm inclined to say that it's a good one.

When Jesus walked the earth, he lived this monumental shift. He never penciled anyone in. He never controlled his time or used it as manipulation to feed his ego—to pat himself on the back and say, "Good, Jesus. Way to go, giving that beggar, that cripple, that Samaritan some of my time. What a good Jesus I am." Instead, Jesus received others as they arrived on the scene of his whereabouts, and he considered their time as a gift given to him.

This consideration is tenderly displayed in his interaction at Jacob's well with the Samaritan woman. Her thirst led her there. His thirst kept her there and kept him there as well. In giving Christ her time, she did more than abate his dehydration. She gave him her story. She stoked the fires of personal relationship when giving Jesus a portion of her day. He received her time as a gift laced with eternal significance. It was a gift of lasting worthiness, not just for the woman but also for those who knew her and for the Father who longs to be known by his children.

Jesus respected the time and the stories of those he met along his way and always considered the human heart above his own. No exchange between Christ and humanity has ever been wasted. It was true two thousand years ago; it's still true today. He sees our time as a gift given to him, and he is well blessed by our willingness to pause at the

Rethinking Time

well for refreshment. Jesus lives the shift I'm now adopting as my own. He authored it. God intends for all of us to move past the notion that our time is a gift that we give to others. Instead, he wants us to live our earthly lives as he lived his: not giving time but receiving time as a gracious bestowment.

So I ask you to rethink your time. Consider the events that you've penciled into your today—the interchanges with humanity, regardless of the conditions surrounding those exchanges. Would you be willing to shift your thinking regarding your time? To view it not as a gift you're giving but rather as a gift you're receiving? If so, if you can make it past the point of selfish intent, then what is your responsibility for that measured portion of time? How will you invest your half of the equation? Will you litter it with lesser words that seed evil rather than good, or will you grace it with sweet thankfulness for being the privileged recipient of the gift?

Not everyone will be able to make this shift. Your time is a final vestige of control. But there are some of you who get it. There are some of you who are ready to cast away previously held pride surrounding your personal time and its investment. Some of you stand ready to consider human hearts above your own. If that's you, then you are ripe for a soul shift of eternal significance.

This may just be the one you're waiting for. It's changing the way I look at all of life, especially those encounters that arrive on the scene of my whereabouts. Rarely are they planned, but always, they can be meaningful. As Jesus lived two thousand years ago, I want to live today—giving the best of myself to others. I imagine you would voice the same. To get to our best, we must begin with a posture of humility, and we must be willing to rethink our time. The greatest gift we can give to others, perhaps, is not our time but the realization that their time is a gift to us. It is a gift not to be wasted but unwrapped, enjoyed, lingered upon, and celebrated.

This is a soul shift indeed. Thus, I pray:

Give us a heart like yours, Father, one that is willing to rethink time and to remove any selfish motives attached therein. Thank you for those who are willing to give us a portion of their days. Grant us the eyes to see their time as a generous gift and a sacred trust to be treated with respect. Even when the encounters are not what we expected, especially when they are unpleasant, help us, Lord, to surrender our expectations and to minister to the hurting heart. Make this soul shift a forever shift in us. Amen.

Living Forward

- How do you view time—as a gift you give to others or as their gift to you?

- Take time to write down a few of the encounters you've had with others in the last twenty-four hours (think broadly to include phone calls, correspondence, and face-to-face exchanges). Which category best describes each of those encounters: *something I needed to do, something he/she needed to do,* or *something we both wanted to do*?

- Now rethink time and take your motives out of the equation. What potential gifts do you see hidden in the exchanges noted above that you had missed?

- Read the following scriptures, and record how they reflect this soul shift. Consider time from both vantage points.

    - Mark 14:3–9
    - John 4:1–26
    - Acts 8:26–40

33

Pressing On

Not that I have already obtained all this, or have already been made perfect, but I press on to take hold of that for which Christ Jesus took hold of me . . . I press on toward the goal to win the prize for which God has called me heavenward in Christ Jesus.
—Philippians 3:12, 14

"PUSH YOURSELF, ELAINE. With each new day, push yourself a little more. Soon, you'll be running again."

So said my oncologist a month after I finished my chemo. I'm afraid his expectations regarding "soon" haven't matched up with my reality. It's now been six months since his proclamation, and I've barely pushed myself past a brisk walk. Every now and again, I manage to add a few strides of slow jogging into my daily routine, but mostly, I walk. The peripheral neuropathy (numbness in my legs and feet) resulting from my chemotherapy has prevented me from moving very fast. With most cancer patients, neuropathy is temporary, but sometimes it lingers . . . sometimes indefinitely. I hope not to fall into the latter category, but as long as it doesn't get any worse, I can live with this. I just may not run again, not the way that I used to run. Twenty-five years of running is a hard habit to break. And so, as I rethink time, as in the previous chapter, I must also rethink my running.

August 27, 2010, was the date of my last good run, a send-off of sorts. With my double mastectomy just a few days away, I knew that running would not be part of my recovery plan. Accordingly, those moments of feeling the pavement beneath my feet were sacred to me. In the quiet and gentle lull of my routine, I handed over my flesh to God. Throughout my earthly tenure, I've come to the altar in the matter of my flesh on many occasions. Time and again, God has been faithful to gather up my remnants and cradle them as his own. On that hot July afternoon, he tenderly gathered them again, both of us knowing what the next few days would mean for me.

Today, I look back on it all with some sadness. That particular surrender was more difficult than previous ones. Not only did I forfeit a pound or two of my flesh, but I also released my lifelong discipline of running. Other surrenders would follow—all very costly, yet all very necessary—but these were the first indicators of the price that would be paid in order that I might live. And I am grateful for the hard work of my healing, for everything I've had to let go of in order to take hold of all that Christ has for me. More of him; less of me. "Then he called the crowd to him along with his disciples and said: 'If anyone would come after me, he must deny himself and take up his cross and follow me. For whoever wants to save his life will lose it, but whoever loses his life for me and for the gospel will save it'" (Mark 8:34–35).

My cross, my back; his cross, his back—flesh surrendered so that life might be saved, so that the gospel, the truth of the truest surrender, might be found in the midst of suffering. Not in surrendering for surrendering's sake but for God's sake. If I'm going to suffer, then I'm going to do so in the shadow of Calvary, where beam meets beam and where the blood bleeds eternal. To suffer without this understanding is to waste the opportunity. To get to the end of all of this and not be changed because of it? What tragedy! What sorrow! What regret! What point?

So my sadness is tempered by reason, by knowing that every chosen surrender made to date has been done with the witness of the cross as my backdrop. I've let go of a great many things, but what I've taken hold of in return far surpasses any temporal loss. Yes, there is less of me these days. With my less, God becomes more. He is seen more, loved more, talked about more, and celebrated more. Not that I have already obtained all of this or been made perfect, but like the apostle Paul, I press onward for more of Jesus. I push myself a little more each day toward the prize that awaits my faith at the end of this road. I may cross the finish line with some numbness in my feet, but my heart will be and is fully sensitized to the joyful realization of what awaits me at the conclusion.

Oh, the marvelous revelation of where our feet are carrying us! Do you understand where the path is winding? That the more steps you take in God's direction, the more enveloped you become in his marvelous light? The less of us reveals more of God. Certainly, there's a price to be paid for surrender, but the exchange of what we're given in return does not balance out in comparison. The scales always tip in favor of the kingdom.

Today, when I return to the streets to walk where my feet once ran, I'll do so with no regrets. Running was my good companion for a long season. Walking is a good companion for me to finish my journey home. It doesn't matter how we get there, friends. Whether we run there, walk there, crawl there, or are carried there by the strong and gracious hold of our Savior. What matters is that we press on in faith with the prize in mind and that we finish the race with God alongside us.

It's going to be something, and it's not going to be long. Keep to the road; I'll meet you at the finish line. Thus, I pray:

Let not the numbness of our flesh and of our hearts keep us from finishing the race, Lord. We are weary travelers, having lost most of our possessions along the way. The beams across our backs are heavy laden and feel like death to us. We need the witness of your cross—your surrender—to better help us carry our own. Strengthen our weakened knees, and straighten the path before us so that we might finish strong. Keep us hidden beneath the cross that we carry so that more of you shines forth as an everlasting witness. Humbly we surrender our flesh for the journey ahead. Amen.

Living Forward

- Consider some of the difficult surrenders you've had to make as you've pressed on in the journey of faith. How have they aided you in your healing process? How have they hindered you?

- Has there ever been a point when you felt that your surrender and subsequent consequences didn't balance evenly? If so, what kept you pressing through?

Beyond the Scars: Daring to Live Forward

- Describe someone in your life (past or present) who has pressed on in faith despite debilitating suffering. How does his or her witness strengthen you as you press on toward the prize for which God has called you?

- Read of Paul's suffering as found in 2 Corinthians 11:16–12:10. What was Paul's great hope in the midst of his weakness (12:9)? How does this same hope encourage you today?

34

Seasons Change

There is a time for everything, and a season for every activity under heaven.
—Ecclesiastes 3:1

I'M CAUGHT UP in King Solomon's beautiful rendering about the seasons of our lives. There are eight poetic verses about time, about rethinking and reframing time in the context of the seasonal soul shifts that seem to arrive naturally within our hearts. One season after another comes, unforced by human manipulation and flowing cyclically in and out of our lives as certain expectations rather than as potentialities.

I read his thoughts and try to pin my current season to one of his. I'm unable to do so, because I find myself in all of them. There are words about:

- life and death,
- planting and uprooting,
- killing and healing,
- tearing down and building up,
- weeping and laughing,
- mourning and dancing,
- scattering and gathering,
- embracing and refraining,
- searching and giving up,
- keeping and throwing away,

- silence and speaking,
- loving and hating,
- wartime and peacetime.

How can I, a cancer survivor, not tag each one of these to my recent growing season? I'm written into every line, in all acts of surrender. In every yielding, I walk my paces and allow my heart the gracious work of the moment. I am emerging into the fuller version of me because of my strong willingness to keep in step with the movement of the shifting wind that cradles my soul.

The wind has most recently carried me through my winter. I name it so because *winter* best describes the elements that were at work in my heart. Hidden beneath the cold and barrenness of winter's grip, new life was forming. My heart was changing. Spring was thinking while winter was doing. In tandem, they produced in me an appreciation for their seasonal work in my life. Some workings can only take place in a winter landscape; some only in spring, summer, or fall. Seasons need room enough to birth their finished work. Accordingly, we must not hurry through them, even when it seems we'd be better off fast forwarding to the next one.

Today, I reflected on my winter season while walking my customary three miles in ninety-degree temperatures. I left my earphones and music at home. For the first time in a long time, I could hear myself think. Silence has been God's very good gift to me in this time of isolation. Without distraction and without schedule, I began thinking about winter's work in my heart and the wind's breath that has carried me along through it.

Winter's work . . . I saw evidence of it while making my trek around the neighborhood. Brittle, brown leaves lined the gutters, skittering along behind me, in front of me, and all around me at the whim of the wind. A lovely sound, a gentle tapping of the pavement reminding me of winter's toll on their previous vitality. And even though their green has faded, their moisture has gone, and their lushness has diminished to dryness, their occupancy on the street remains despite their replacements shading my steps. Their brittle and brown are still lovely to me. They're still shapely, still intricate in their design, and a memorial to an earlier season.

Wind's breath . . . a carrier of brittle things, lighter things, and things that have allowed winter its witness within them. The wind cannot carry what is heavily tethered to earth. Whether it's a leaf, a blossom, a bird, or a heart, when life stays attached to worldliness, life will never know the uplift of the wind—the soaring, gentle, gracious rise of heaven's breath—a memorial to an eternal truth that says there comes a:

Seasons Change

- Going down before a going up.
- Drying up before a flying high.
- Letting go before a being held.
- Tender fall before a gracious lift.
- Sacred burial before a sacred resurrection.
- Winter's work before a spring's revival.

Indeed, my thoughts had room enough to think today, just enough to serve as a reminder to me that all has not been lost in my winter, that despite the drying up of this season, I have retained my occupancy upon this earth. I'm still intricate in my design, still retaining the veins and shape of an earlier season, still here amid the heat of my summer, yet lighter now because of the stripping of winter.

Like my leafy friends, I'm better able to rise with the wind's breath because of winter's work within me—a going-down, drying-up, letting-go, tender-falling, sacred-burial kind of work—a vigorous requirement of my flesh and in regards to my faith. Winter seasons can be rigid and unrelenting at times, forcing their agenda, offering no apologies. I've had no need to ask for one.

As with the seasons on earth, so it is with our hearts. We cannot forego winter in favor of spring, summer, or fall. We simply must receive the seasons as they arrive, believing that "there is a time for everything, and a season for every activity under heaven" (Eccles. 3:1). Winter holds a wealth all its own, and today, I briefly caught a glimpse of its worthiness. I heard it as well—skittering leaves pushed along and lifted up by the wind. Winter's work and heaven's breath; winter's labor and heaven's grace—what generous kindness to hold as my comfort and hope!

I don't know what season you're walking through, but I do know that each one bares a worthiness all its own. As you trace the heart of King Solomon, I imagine that you, along with me, are able to find the lines of your story tangled up with each line of his. There's hope to be found there, to our realizing that we live a seasonal faith and that, with that living, comes a time for every thing—every joy, pain, frustration, surrender, sorrow, and celebration. Nothing in our lives is exempt from the cyclical process of our emerging into fuller, better versions of ourselves. We may refuse the seasonal work of winter, spring, summer, and fall. We can choose to walk through them with little or no effect to our hearts, but we cannot deny the possibility of growth extended to us because of them. Each season of our lives is rife with eternal possibilities. The soul shift happens when we bow low and lean into those possibilities.

Beyond the Scars: Daring to Live Forward

Winter has been the soil of my recent soul shift. It has been cold, brutal, and unrelenting at times. But it has produced a stronger spirit in me. I hope you can say the same of your season. Thus, I pray:

Do your work in us, Lord, no matter the season that cradles our steps. Give us eyes to see its worthiness, and grant us a willing spirit to cede our hearts to its working. Carry us along by the wind of your Spirit, and remind us of your accompanying grace that follows after us as we go. You make everything beautiful in its time, even our winters. Lend us your strength as we patiently await spring's arrival. Amen.

Living Forward

- In what season are you currently living (winter, spring, summer, or fall)? What characteristics make it so?

- When did you last walk through a wintering season? What perspective, healing, or gift came to you because of that seasonal work?

- Read Solomon's witness as found in Ecclesiastes 3:1–22. Where do you find your heart most closely aligned to his? What hope can you claim as personal treasure from this passage?

35

Live On

And yet we live on.

—2 Corinthians 6:9

MY SEASONAL ACHE. My winter ache. My heartache. My temporal ache. It's been with me for nearly a year now. This has been the one season of my life that has authored an unusual amount of connection between the faith I boldly proclaim and the steps required to walk that faith. It's a daily choice to merge the two realities, and I'm not always successful at doing so. But I try, knowing that I don't receive a pass on this one. Not really. Not if I want to fully engage with my life and my spiritual maturity therein. And when I get to the end of my daily doing, when the lights go out and I most profoundly feel the ache of a day's worth of obedience, I am reminded of an important truth regarding the call of Jesus Christ upon my life.

Kingdom work is sometimes flanked by the painful ache of a sacred obedience.

If we are Christians, if we dare to name ourselves with the name of our Lord and Savior, Jesus Christ, then we are to be heartily invested in his kingdom business. It's his *mandate* to us, not a suggestion. Vocationally speaking, we may hold a variety of titles behind our names, but spiritually speaking, the only holding of our hearts that matters is the God who titles us as his. And when we get this, when we finally arrive at the place of realizing that all of our earthly endeavors are meant to be the fertile soil upon which the King sows his seed, then we readily accept the fullness of that calling—ills, aches, and cancer included.

Beyond the Scars: Daring to Live Forward

The apostle Paul understood the strain between a painful ache and a sacred obedience. He willingly chose his ache, chaining himself to the gospel of Jesus Christ and believing that every temporal pain of his flesh was achieving for him an eternal glory that far outweighed them all. At any point along the way, Paul could have chosen otherwise. He could have freed himself from the physical and emotional misery that invaded his flesh. Instead, he persevered in great travail and suffering so that the church might know the culminating truth of the cross, so that the church would grow, so that you and I, some two thousand years down the road, might know what it is to live on despite the carnage and chaos presently rummaging through our lives. But don't take my word on it; take his:

> Rather, as servants of God we commend ourselves in every way: in great endurance; in troubles, hardships and distresses; in beatings, imprisonments and riots; in hard work, sleepless nights and hunger; in purity, understanding, patience and kindness; in the Holy Spirit and in sincere love; in truthful speech and in the power of God; with weapons of righteousness in the right hand and in the left; through glory and dishonor, bad report and good report; genuine, yet regarded as impostors; known, yet regarded as unknown; dying, and yet we *live on*; beaten, and yet not killed; sorrowful, yet always rejoicing; poor, yet making many rich; having nothing, and yet possessing everything. (2 Corinthians 6:4–10, emphasis added)

I'd never seen it before—Paul's "live on." When reading this familiar passage, I'm tempted to stay mired in the pain of it all, imagining how my own life fits into the litany of sufferings he vividly details in his letter to the church at Corinth. Yet they're there—two simple words that admonished readers back then and admonish readers right now to live on; to refuse to stay entrenched in the ache of obedience to Jesus Christ but to live on in spite of it; to keep putting one spiritual foot of faith in front of the other until we press through to victory and realize, even as Paul realized, that we possess everything, even though the world labels our possession as nothing.

It's the painful ache of a sacred obedience.

Some of you are living your ache today. Some of you are all too familiar with Paul's suffering because yours, at some level, mirrors his. You may not be locked in a prison cell or experiencing the physical trauma of a flogging, but I imagine there are many of you who feel the emotional and spiritual intensity of some chains, some wearing and tearing away of your flesh that feels comparable in depth to Paul's.

Some of you are expending a lot of your faith on behalf of God's kingdom while seeing little results. Some of you are standing on the front line of a tenacious, spiritual battle in which the line is wearing thin and your reserves have run for cover, leaving you alone to fight it through to victory. Some of you are tired; sleepless nights have claimed your good

Live On

sense, and the energy for a new day has long since been usurped by the previous night's wanderings of your mind. Some of you are hungry; a famine of soul is crying out for the bread of heaven, yet the manna seems to have missed your acreage during its morning dispensation. Some of you are working hard, enduring long, speaking truth, and loving lavishly, yet the payoff seems minimal and our Father's notice all the more minimal. You feel unknown and like an imposter upon the soil beneath your feet.

I hear you. I feel you. I cannot fully understand what it is like to be you, but I too have known moments, days, and this most recent season of feeling the ache of my obedience. I cannot perfectly aid your comprehension as it pertains to the questions and whys behind your struggle, but I can, like the apostle Paul, give to you a couple of words that have carried me through this suffering season.

"Live on."

Don't die midstream. Live on. Press through. Receive everything as if it were happening to our Lord Jesus Christ, and then, live on. For of this I am certain: you are known by our heavenly Father. He sees your sacred obedience and regards your faith as genuine in his eyes. If you remain faithful to live on in Jesus, despite personal suffering, then there is nothing in your past, present, or future that will be able to undercut the witness of God's kingdom in your flesh. Nothing. You can live on because Christ lives on. So did Paul; so have countless unnamed others who have gone before you, who will follow after you, and who, in this moment, stand beside you to cheer you on toward victory.

I am one of them, friends. We are on the kingdom road together. God intends for us to be here and to love one another in the strength and power of his Holy Spirit . . . to live on together until we move home to heaven. It is but a moment from now—a single breath that will transport us into our "next," where our living on will live on in living color before the very face of God. Believing and fully trusting in that moment brings me rich perspective for the temporal aches I experience. All of them can be connected to a kingdom end that far outweighs my momentary striving, to God's kingdom end. What better end is there to end on? Thus, I pray:

> *Jesus, keep me obedient to live on. Draw my attention away from the pains that assail me, and plant my thoughts on higher ground. You are that higher ground, and you have a purpose for this season I've walked through. Grant me wisdom and understanding as I search out that purpose, and draw me closer to your heart. Thank you for your living on. Because you do so, I can do the same. Amen.*

Beyond the Scars: Daring to Live Forward

Living Forward

- Identify the painful ache of your obedience. What has it required of you?

- Reread Paul's words from 2 Corinthians 6:4–10. What line best fits with your current season of living? Why?

- What does Paul's "live on" mean for you? What are some of the obstacles you are facing as you endeavor to live on?

- Take some time to linger on some additional thoughts from Paul in 2 Corinthians 4:1–18. How does this passage add purpose and meaning to your living on?

36

Be Prepared to Give an Answer

But in your hearts set apart Christ as Lord. Always be prepared to give an answer to everyone who asks you to give the reason for the hope that you have.

—1 Peter 3:15

SHE CORNERED ME at my eldest son's college graduation. I was busy taking pictures; she was busy admiring my hair—the recent sprouts of rebirth upon my once-balding scalp.

"Your hair is beautiful. So very attractive on you."

I paused from my picture taking, looked into her sweet eyes, and said, "There's a story that comes with this hair."

Her gracious response was more than I anticipated, yet one with which I was fully prepared to engage: "I thought that might be the case; tell me more."

And so I did. For the next few minutes, I shared with her some of my cancer story, and I told her about the grace and peace of Jesus Christ that have sustained me on my road of suffering. We shared our tears, our hugs as well, and when I left her embrace, I knew that we had been standing on sacred ground—God's ground. There was a pulpit and a preacher, a sermon and a learner, with both of us sharing in dual roles.

Preaching runs in my family. My daddy's a preacher, my husband as well. From time to time, I've been accused of being the same (just ask my children). But what does that title really mean? According to the dictionary, *preaching* means "to deliver a sermon." And *sermon*? "A religious discourse delivered in public usually by a clergyman as a part of a worship service; a speech on conduct or duty."[7] Sounds rather perfunctory, does it not? Sounds rather boring as well.

For most folks, the word *preaching* usually stirs up one of two responses: respect or suspicion. Suspicion because preaching, after all, sounds kind of preachy—kind of proud. Kind of like, "You've got something to learn, and I've got all the answers. Listen to me." Not everyone responds well to that kind of preaching. I understand. While it might be true that I have something to learn, I sometimes have a hard time with those who claim to have all the answers, especially when those answers are framed within the context of their saying, "Listen to me." Where the respect comes is when a preacher moves the focus off of "me" and points it back to God. "Look to Thee, not me." Now that kind of preaching deserves my attention, and it's that kind of preaching God has called each one of us to as his disciples.

We are charged with the dispensing of God's grace and truth, regardless of the stage we're standing upon. This is a weighty responsibility to be certain. You may not think of yourself as a preacher—as someone entrusted with God's story to tell. Perhaps you're having a hard time even putting words to your own story of cross bearing and suffering tears. Throwing a little faith in the mix is the furthest thing from your mind because, quite honestly, faith hasn't been a priority to you as you've tried to manage your pain in isolation.

But God has been there, even when you've been unwilling to acknowledge his presence. Remember Spurgeon's words? "Before we had a being in the world we had a being in His heart."[8] You can spend a lifetime trying to separate yourself from your true identity, but the truth is, your heart is directly connected back to God's heart. Your image? It's made in some likeness to his. There's something about you that resembles your Creator, and the sooner you acknowledge this eternal pulse within you, the sooner your saying, "Listen to me," will count for more than temporal gain. With God as your compass, the sermons you preach and the pulpits you grace will count for all eternity, forming a lasting memorial to a life well lived, well appreciated, and well spoken.

As survivors—whether of cancer or of some other debilitating disease that has sought to claim us and hold us captive—we have the unique privilege of sharing the witness of God's faithfulness to us as we've moved in and out of our suffering. We've stood on the edge of our own mortality and, by the grace of God, have lived another day to tell about it. If God has not been a part of that journey, then the words we offer about survival and finding hope are rooted in selfish motives—in "Listen to me" instead of "Look to Thee." Survival becomes about what we've done for ourselves, without our ever giving consideration to all that God has done for us.

God has done it all, readers. By his unmerited grace and because of his unconditional love for you, you awoke this morning to a new day, to a new pulpit from which to share the reason for the hope you hold in your heart. You may not be willing to give God all the credit he is due, but your unwillingness doesn't change the fact that God is, in fact, due all the credit for every single day of your earthly tenure.

I don't have the answers as to why some of our tenures last longer than others. Indeed, it seems as if far too many lives are cut short, and some, perhaps, last longer than I expected. But not knowing those answers doesn't keep me from living my today. Today is what I've been given—these few moments of time to continue in my testifying about the willing strength of God that has labored on my behalf and carried me to this morning pulpit of grace. He is the sermon worth sharing. Any other mention from our daily pulpits is worthy of suspicion.

In your hearts, set apart Christ as Lord. And should people come asking for more of your story—for the reason behind the hope you hold in your heart—be prepared to give them an answer. Give them Jesus. In doing so, you give them the key to the kingdom.

In lieu of our closing prayer, I'd like to share with you a poem that was written for my husband just days after my mastectomy surgery. I pray it ministers to you as it has ministered to me, a sermon from the pulpit of a humbled preacher known to me as Uncle Bill.

Billy at 43

Lord, it's Sunday morning,
and Billy has to preach—
boy turns 43 on the 10th.
Wife and four children—
facing mighty tough times,
but, Lord, it's Sunday morning,
and Billy has to preach.
Help him to carve out the truth—
the truth from his text
and his subtext. Prayin' for him,
Lord; if he gets the Sunday off,
he'll still be giving it up for others—
man of compassion like this
doesn't shut down when hurtin'—
so, Lord, help this Billy man,
cause on Friday, he turns 43.

Beyond the Scars: Daring to Live Forward

> Lord, when I was 43
> I just done sobered up,
> never coulda faced
> what this preacher man handles—
> a new parish, a family in pain,
> and his own heart broken
> but with a faith that sustains.
> And here we have
> his former parish
> coming out in droves
> to say, "We love ya,"
> and family and friends
> from around the world
> are holding this holy home
> in a protective love that releases
> the deepest cry,
> and it is that cry, Lord,
> that will see us through.
> Yes, as I was sayin'—
> it's Sunday morning, Lord,
> and Billy has to preach.[9]

It's Sunday morning, and we all have to preach! By the grace of God, preach him well. Amen. So be it.

Living Forward

- What venue serves as the pulpit for your preaching in this current season of your life?

- What sermon are you sharing with your listeners? Would they consider it with respect or with suspicion?

Be Prepared to Give an Answer

ଔ What are some of the graces and hope that God has written into your story?

ଔ Read some further words about preaching your story from the apostle Peter's pen as found in 1 Peter 4:1–11. What will be the final sermon of your earthly life?

37

Eden Is Closer Now Than It Has Ever Been

Abraham and Sarah were already old and well advanced in years, and Sarah was past the age of childbearing. So Sarah laughed to herself as she thought, "After I am worn out and my master is old, will I now have this pleasure?"
—Genesis 18:11–12

THE SCENE CAUGHT me off guard. I wasn't expecting it; any expectations I held regarding its arrival had long since evaporated during the five hours of walking in the sweltering June temperatures. My feet were swollen, my shirt drenched in sweat, and my only remaining desire was to find a cold drink and the comfort of our air-conditioned minivan. We had a couple of exhibits left in our survey of the North Carolina Zoo in Asheboro. My family was tempted to skip over them in favor of the coming comfort, but the perfectionist in me—the part that screams, "We must see it all!"—didn't allow them a pass. Instead, we forged ahead through twists and turns and upward asphalt until we rounded a corner and witnessed a scene I will never forget.

At first, it seemed like an exhibit closed for repairs. The patch of upward, sloping field was barren of animals, save for the few frogs visible in the stream of water bordering the exhibit. But then, as if on cue, I spotted some movement at the crest of the hill. Giraffes, zebras, ostriches, all moving in unison, side by side, were descending down the hill and stepping on the pathway toward us. It was an incredibly beautiful moment of grace accompanied by a whisper from heaven: *"Eden is closer now than it has ever been."*

Tears welled in my eyes, my heart as well, making the previous labored moments of heated walking worth the price of admission. To catch a glimpse of Eden on this side of eternity—to stand within arm's reach of my up-and-coming reality—is enough to buoy my faith forward in great anticipation for what awaits me around the next corner. Very few times in my life have I been so enraptured in a moment.

Perhaps I was unable to see clearly in previous seasons. Perhaps in those seasons, seeing Eden felt less necessary, less urgent, less important as it pertained to the temporal urges of the moment. Perhaps, today, I have more time and more willingness to ponder Edenic pleasures. My cancer season has afforded me this gift.

As a forty-four-year-old woman with a new diagnosis of cancer, I felt a bit like my spiritual ancestor Sarah. Old, worn out, and well past the point of having any more children, I thought that my life had pretty much run its course in regards to new pleasures. Routines were set. Patterns of thinking were mostly fixed. Cancer was wearing its witness on me. My heart was certainly open for a fresh work from God, but I never expected this—a new way of thinking and doing my life forever forward.

Sarah laughed at the idea of a new way of doing life. Maybe she even mocked the thought that she, advanced in years and weary from her travels, might now have a new pleasure—the gift of a child, a new life in the midst of her old age. The word *pleasure* in the original language—*adnah*—roots back to the same word used in Genesis 2:8 as the location for the Lord's garden: "Now the Lord God had planted a garden in the east, in Eden; and there he put the man he had formed."

Eden served as the soil for God to exercise his green thumb. Isaac served as an Edenic moment for Sarah and Abraham, and the North Carolina Zoo served as an Edenic moment for me, reminding me of things yet to be. They were moments of pleasure for all of us, moments of realizing that Eden has always been the soil of God's preference, and that, every now and again, we're given a pleasure from his garden to hold as a revelatory grace that threads us back to home.

I will not forget this recent scene from our zoo trip. The creatures were majestic in their gaits and painted with all the creativity of the Creator, who wasn't content to settle for lackluster works of art. Instead, he gave them color and stripes and shapely form, so much so that when I saw them, the only response of my heart was, "Only God could do this, paint this, give this. Only God."

Is anything too hard for the Lord? Is any life too crumpled and rumpled by the passage of time for God to do a new work within? Is anything too wonderful, too marvelous, too surpassing, too extraordinary, too distinguishing for the first Gardener of Eden? If God willingly brought these marvelous creatures to Eden and a son to Sarah in her old age, then what is too much for him to bring to you? Our Father is the author of Edenic pleasures, and your heart is the fertile soil in which he longs to plant them. He desires to

Eden Is Closer Now Than It Has Ever Been

give good gifts to his children. He wants to bring Eden to you—to do a new thing in your life, a larger thing and a better thing than what you're currently believing him for today.

Our God is the God of sacred replacement. He takes the old, weary, worn-out parts of our hearts and supplants them with his new works of mercy and grace. We will never outlive his reach of love, never move so far outside the gates of Eden as to incubate ourselves from its stretching witness. If Eden were reserved solely for the first three chapters of Genesis, then why have we been trying to get back there ever since? Why the holes in our hearts that yearn for filling? The questions in our minds that search for answers? The moral compass that points us eastward, even though our evil inclinations draw us away?

There is a place named Eden, and it is closer now than it has ever been—despite our doubts, despite our wanderings, and despite old age and fragile diseases. Even now, Eden is approaching our souls, and God doesn't want us to miss its arrival. From the crest of a hill it will appear, moving downward onto the barren landscape that cries out for its advent and for the Gardener who is willing to do a new work, plant a new thing, grow a new world, and call it *Eden*.

This is our season to receive a fresh planting from the Lord. Eden is upon us, just beyond the hill in front of us. Wait for it, friends. Don't push past it in favor of temporal pleasures. Instead, linger long enough in the scene, with your eyes cast to the horizon in expectation of its unveiling. As it comes, it will be a scene to enrapture us for all eternity.

Only God could do this, paint this, give this. Only God. Even so, come Lord Jesus. Thus, I pray:

Bring Eden to our hearts, Father, as we stand ready to receive its unveiling. We long for more of its witness in our daily lives. We need reminders of the goodness and perfection that lived back then. They move us forward in our faith and bring anticipation to our hearts for our eternal home. Like Sarah, we sometimes wonder if the pleasure we desire is too much for you to handle, too much grace for our sin-sick hearts. Forgive us when we reason our desires in light of our perceptions about what you do and don't do for us. Eden is yours to give. Eden is ours to receive. Merge these truths as a solid anchor for our faith today. Amen.

Beyond the Scars: Daring to Live Forward

Living Forward

- When has a momentary pleasure reminded you of the beauty of Eden?

- What one pleasure—one thing—in your life right now seems too hard for the Lord?

- Why is it sometimes difficult to move past suffering to take hold of the new work that God longs to do in your heart?

- Read Sarah and Abraham's story in its entirety as found in Genesis 18:1–15; 21:1–7. Record the many steps that God took to bring Isaac into their lives. What do you learn about God from these passages?

38

God Will Take You Across the River

> *Then Moses went out and spoke these words to all Israel: "I am now a hundred and twenty years old and I am no longer able to lead you. The L*ORD *has said to me, 'You shall not cross the Jordan.' The L*ORD *your God himself will cross over ahead of you . . . . The L*ORD *himself goes before you and will be with you; he will never leave you nor forsake you. Do not be afraid; do not be discouraged."*
> —Deuteronomy 31:1–3, 8

AS I NEAR the end of this writing project, there is a lump in my throat, my heart as well. I've been saving this particular writing for a few weeks now, reserving it for a time such as this—an almost-ending time. This thought seared through to my heart one evening while I was out taking a walk with my daughter. It is a heart truth that simply and profoundly says, "God will take you across the river."

Let me explain. As our walks usually go, my nine-year-old daughter rides her bike while I pitifully endeavor to keep up with her pace. She's usually far ahead of me; I'm mostly fine with her taking the lead as long as she follows this one, simple rule: she must wait for me before "crossing the river."

The river—that's the term we use to describe the intersections of streets in our neighborhood, including the corners and the stopping points where we "look both ways before crossing the street." She isn't allowed to move forward with that crossing until I give her the go-ahead.

"Wait for me, Amelia, before crossing the river."

She's always faithful to wait, always eager to move ahead, but willing to linger for her mother's official word. Funny thing: she constantly arrives at the crossings before I do, at least until a few weeks ago, when I beat her. She had stopped her forward motion to remove a pebble from her shoe; I kept moving while she did surgery. I could hear her saying, "Wait for me!" as I moved along. Her words didn't stop me, but then she said something that did.

"Mommy, please wait for me before crossing the river. You can't cross the river without me."

Like a bolt of lightning from God's heart to mine, I was struck by the profundity of her words. I couldn't move. Instead, I just cried, and when she arrived at my side and inquired about the reason behind my tears, I spoke some truth over her precious, young heart. "There may come a day, sweet one, when you'll have to cross this river without me. But rest assured, God will walk it with you. He's gone ahead of us both, and he'll make sure that we land safely on the other side."

It seemed enough of a reason to quell her curiosity in that moment; although, I'm certain she didn't feel the ground beneath her feet shaking in the same way I felt it quaking. Her heart's not quite ready to undertake the weightiness of such truth. Nevertheless, I spoke it, and today I write it, believing that somewhere down the road, she'll retrieve this memory from my pen and better understand the fullness of what I'm saying—how I'm trying to live my life faith forward, with not a single crumb of doubt left in my wake.

Whenever that day comes for me—my crossing-over day—I don't want there to be any lingering questions as to what I believed and where I'm headed. Mind you, I'm not in much of a hurry to take on the Jordan River, not yet. My heart is still closely attached to the promises I'm living on this side of Canaan. The life I share with my husband and my four children is a good life to live. It is a life worth fighting for, and then, as God so chooses, a life to lay down in favor of the greener pastures and perfect promises of the land just beyond this one—a home across the river.

Until then, I want to fully live each day as it arrives. I want to give my children some years, some more time to get grown and get established in their faith. I want to be part of that shaping process. In addition, I am committed to the earthly tenure I've been given. Life is a precious gift and worth preserving. God created me with a purpose in mind, and for as long as I have breath, I am wholly devoted to that purpose—to know God more with each passing day and then, out of that knowing, to lead others to know the same. Kingdom truth can march on without me, but it feels right and good and sacred to be part of the story—the telling of it and living it therein.

Yes, I still have some earthly attachments. Life on this side of the river has been a good landscape in which to grow my kingdom heart. I'll keep walking the streets with my daughter and crossing the rivers with her for as long as I'm given the privilege. But I'll always do so with an eye fixed on forever. I'll keep telling her about Canaan, keep reminding her about home and about the God who has crossed all rivers in front of her, making certain of her safe arrival on the other side. It's what I must do. It's all I know to do. It's how I must live—fully committed to the journey at large.

I don't know where you are today. Maybe you're standing on the edge of your Jordan, preparing your heart for a difficult crossing. Maybe you're far away from the water's edge, riding your bike and keeping pace with limited understanding. Maybe, like I am, you're somewhere in between, approaching the river, yet still far enough a way that you have time for further conversations—important living words that impart God's kingdom seed into the soil of a future generation. Wherever you are, today is still today, and there is still time to take the hand of Jesus and trust him with the crossing that's ahead.

God will take you across the river. No one else can. No one else deserves the privilege, because no one else can land you safely on the other side. I cannot carry you there any more than I can carry my daughter with me as I go. I can only point you to the one who can. The one who has walked it before us and whose name is written on the deed to Canaan. Only God can offer such glorious hope to our wounded, fearful, and often discouraged hearts. Canaan is God's Promised Land to give. And because of his Son's surrender to a cross, we all have a share in that inheritance.

Today's a good day to take a walk with someone you love. Take the lead, or fall in step behind, but as you arrive at the "rivers" along your path, take a hand. Cross the river together, and remember the hand and heart of the one who has crossed it before you.

God will take you across the river, readers. And should we never meet on this side of the Jordan, I'll be standing on the shores of Canaan, awaiting your arrival. Safe passage. Keep to the road of faith. Thus, I pray:

To stand at the Jordan and look over to Canaan, Lord, is a glorious revelation of grace. Thank you for all the reminders of promise that come to us; they help us move forward with perspective. Canaan seems so far in coming, yet we know it's but a moment from now. Thank you for crossing the river ahead of us, for making our path straight, and for securing our safe passage prior to our departure. Father, our attachments to our earthly tenures are strong, sometimes we're unwilling to let go of them because of the pain attached to the release. Temper the pain with the truth of what awaits us, and gladden our hearts with expectation for the forever that we will share together. Amen.

Beyond the Scars: Daring to Live Forward

Living Forward

- What fears do you hold about your eternal crossing of the Jordan River to reach Canaan? What hopes?

- How does the witness of the Lord going before you, and the witness of countless others going before you, strengthen your heart for the crossing over that you will one day make?

- What special people are joining you on your journey toward Canaan? What gifts are you giving to them and receiving from them as you travel together?

- Even though Moses wouldn't be allowed to lead the Israelites through the Jordan, into the Promised Land, he had his own crossing over with the Lord. Read about it in Deuteronomy 34:1–12. What special gift did God give to Moses in their time together on Mount Nebo?

39

God Is Next

After this, the word of the LORD came to Abram in a vision: "Do not be afraid, Abram. I am your shield, your very great reward."
—Genesis 15:1

I HOLD AN eighteen-month-old remembrance in my heart today. Eighteen months ago, I was sitting in my dining room, looking out the window at the cars passing by in front of our home. Life was crowding in on me. Moving boxes filled up our living space, along with the thirty-two boxes that had recently arrived, containing copies of my first book, *Peace for the Journey*. I had marketing work to do for my book and moving work to do for my family. In a couple of months, we'd be leaving our church for a new ministry opportunity. Just over an hour's drive separated one place from the other, but the transition would require much more than an hour's worth of labor.

The bulging dreams I held in my heart for this new chapter in my life were surpassed only by the bulging realities of what needed to be accomplished in order to start living those dreams. It was a lot to take on—this merging of dreams with reality. Still, I wanted to be wholly invested in the process, knowing that the greater my investment on the front side of dreaming, the greater my return somewhere down the road.

Accordingly, I welcomed my boxes and all the stresses that tenaciously attached themselves to the packing and unpacking of a new life. I sat in the midst of them that March morning and spent some time talking to God about the road ahead. Mainly, I asked him a few simple questions, never anticipating the response that I would receive.

"God, what's next for me? What's awaiting my arrival in our new town? What dreams? What new realities? What can I expect as a reward to this forward-moving faith of mine? Lord, what's next?"

Have you ever been there? Ever wanted to know what your "up ahead" is going to look like before it arrives? Ever asked God for a sneak peek into your future? Further still, have you ever received an answer from him in response to your questions? I received one that day.

As clearly as I have ever heard the voice of the Father in my spirit, he pressed his answer into my heart: *"I'm next, Elaine. I'm your next."*

His words stun me today, even as they stunned me back then. God as my "next"? There's little to do with a response like that, except to say, "Yes!" and, "Amen!" and, "Let's get moving on with my next!" That's what I told him eighteen months ago, sitting among the boxes. That's what I tell him today. Between my then and my now, there's been an unfolding of reality I hadn't imagined on the front side of our move: my cancer reality. It's not even been a year since I received my diagnosis. It feels like a year, maybe more like ten years' worth of hard living. But through it all, I've clung to the truth of my next—my Savior, Jesus Christ. His words of promise from eighteen months ago have served as rich salve to my recent woundings and have brought hope to me on days when I felt like my next might not ever arrive.

Today, as I consider my walk of faith, I am reminded of Abraham's walk as well. He was mired down in the middle of his next—stuck in between the eternal promises given to him by God in Genesis 12 and the fruition of those promises beginning in Genesis 21. In between those bookends were nine chapters of tested faith—twenty-five years of wandering in and out of the accompanying frustrations that attach themselves to a willing trust. These were realities he hadn't planned on when he was packing up his old life and moving forward with God into new territory. Perhaps you understand. I know I certainly do. From the time I began my walk with Jesus Christ up until today, there have been many challenges to my faith and many frustrations to point their fingers in the face of my belief, to mock my certain assurances, and to dare me to let go of the hope I so boldly proclaim.

Like Abraham, I get stuck some days—weighed down in the middle of my own nine chapters. Rescuing my "Lot" from the fires of Sodom and from the clutches of earthly kings can be exhausting. All I really want to do is to arrive on the other side of conflict in order to live peacefully in the land of God's promises, but it seems there's always another "something" standing in my way. Another obstacle placed in between previously spoken promises and promises fulfilled. Another testing. Another wrestling. Another refining. Another day to live out the convictions of my faith—none more so than the days of my last year.

Like my next from God, Abraham received a strong encouragement from the Lord in the midst of his moving faith: "Do not be afraid, Abram. I am your shield, your very great reward."

I don't know how God's response to me and his response to Abraham weigh out in comparison, but I'm thinking that "I'm next" and "I am your very great reward" stand side by side as a great grace given to anyone walking the struggling road of faith. If God were not our reward—our next—then what is the point of our faith? If there is nothing to be gained from our allegiance to an unseen God, then why bother with religious formality? Why not just take our lumps, make the best out of a bad situation—eat, drink, and be merry until life ends at the grave? If there is no next with Jesus, then there is no hope for any of us. Just more of the same, constantly running into the dead end of discouragement.

Christians, it's time to start living with the hope of our next. Hope isn't rooted in the seen and tangible rewards of this life. Hope is rooted in the eternal gift of heaven—in Bethlehem's joy, in Calvary's cry, in Easter's coronation. Jesus Christ, Son of the living God, our very good and great reward, he is my next, and he is enough, no matter the boxes I unpack today or the boxes that arrive on my doorstep tomorrow. God is the hope to be unwrapped in them all. Thus, I pray:

Thank you for your answer that comes to us, Lord, in the midst of our dreaming and questions about our tomorrows. You are the answer. You are The Way, The Truth, The Life. You are heaven's gracious gift to us as we walk out steps of faith. Forgive us for thinking that there should be more—that knowing you and daily living with you isn't enough of a reward. You are the author and perfecter of our faith. The work that you began in us so long ago, you will bring to completion in time. Until then, help us to rest peacefully in your presence. You are our next, and you are enough. Amen.

Living Forward

◦ What are some of the questions you have about your "next"?

◦ What promises has God spoken over your life that are yet to be fully realized?

Beyond the Scars: Daring to Live Forward

- How does realizing that Jesus is your next better help you to frame the realities you are living with today?

- Read God's initial promise to Abraham in Genesis 12:2–3. Briefly glance at the events that occurred between that time and the time of Isaac's birth in Genesis 21. What were some of the major hurdles that Abraham faced during those twenty-five years?

- Read John 14:15–27. How does this passage parallel the truth that Christ is our next and our very great reward?

40

God Is Faithful

> *But as surely as God is faithful, our message to you is not "Yes" and "No."*
> *For the Son of God, Jesus Christ, who was preached among you by me and Silas*
> *and Timothy, was not "Yes" and "No," but in him it has always been "Yes."*
> *For no matter how many promises God has made, they are "Yes" in Christ.*
> *And so through him the "Amen" is spoken by us to the glory of God.*
> —2 Corinthians 1:18–20

I DO BELIEVE that there are some promises that God has spoken over each one of us in advance of their coming to fruition in our lives, some words of grace and holy impartation that he speaks on our behalf prior to their unfolding witness. Rarely are we aware of these sacred declarations; not because God doesn't long to make them obvious to us, but rather because our eyes are often glazed over by the temporal scenes that surround us. But every now and again, we become attentive to God's whispers. We understand his intentions up front, and we watch in holy expectation for his words to unfold as living truth.

Forty days ago, God announced a few words to my heart, and I heard them in my spirit as clearly as I hear the fan humming in my bedroom this afternoon. "Out of your poverty, Elaine, surrender your pen."

Today, forty days beyond his declaration, I can barely push the pen across the paper. There's a holy hush in my spirit. Sacred ground swells beneath my feet, and the strong witness of Jesus Christ is all around me. I've come to the end of this work of grace, for that is what it has been: a grace given to me from the God who always keeps his promises.

Beyond the Scars: Daring to Live Forward

When I started this writing project, I didn't know if I had any words left in me, much less sixty thousand of them. I certainly didn't have a great deal of confidence in my writing ability, and my emotions were at their rawest, lowest level. I don't ever remember a time in my life when I've felt so wrung out, so very aware of my poverty, so tired, and so ready for something to change—for something to move, for someone to do something for me that I wasn't able to do for myself.

I needed to be rescued, not from breast cancer but from a second, less detectable diagnosis that resulted from my first one. A "cancer" that had nothing to do with my breasts and everything to do with my heart. I needed rescuing from the hopelessness and despair that had found their way into my heart after a season of suffering. Picking up and putting on a new life after an old one has died is a difficult exchange, especially when scars and painful memories remain.

Yes, the surgeries and treatments were rigorous, thorough, and unrelenting at times, leaving their own marks across my flesh. They did what they needed to do in order to preserve my life for a season longer. But in their wake, they forgot to bandage the resulting emotional pain that nearly shattered my heart, mind, and soul into a thousand pieces. Those wounds were left open, vulnerable to the prodding influence of the enemy, whose only intent is to steal, kill, and destroy—to pour salt into open wounds in hopes of irreparably damaging the soul. That is where I was forty days ago—on the verge of collapse.

Friends and well-meaning doctors told me that it would take time to heal, that six months from my last six months, and six months from now, I'd feel more like myself again. And while I understand the worthiness of what they said, I'm not sure their prediction is accurate. I will never feel like my old self again. The old self is gone; behold, the new is upon me. I have little use for my flesh anymore, except that it serves as my outer covering to hold my inward parts together so God can carry me forward to minister his kingdom purposes.

When we are able to get to this point of surrender—when we cede the ownership of our flesh back into the hands of the one who created it—then we are saved, truly rescued from ourselves. We are healed in a holy way that places us in close proximity to the beating pulse of God's heart and his intentions for our lives. When we, out of our poverty, cast our final coppers into God's temple treasury, then our hearts are never more pure before him. God can use hearts like that. Poverty is indeed a good starting point for the rich increase of the Father's grace and healing. This is where I began forty days ago, and today, God completes this chapter of my healing process.

Here's the rub. Forty days ago, I didn't fully realize the bankruptcy that existed within me, and I certainly didn't comprehend what my daily obedience to write would yield. I

God Is Faithful

only knew my desperation and had an inclination that my pen was somehow connected to the process of my healing. It's been no small thing, readers. It's been huge. Whether or not my words mean much to you in your season of struggle, they've been the means that God has used to pour his ministering rain into my heart. I am reminded today of those initial questions I wrote forty days ago: "Will they be enough, Lord? Are these words worth fighting for? Is there ample ink left in my well—enough words and enough willingness—to write this chapter of my story? Will this surrender be costly? Will the end result reflect the fight required to get there? Will joy replace current sorrow? Will fullness replace this emptiness I'm holding? Will hope supplant doubt? Will kingdom work be done through weakness?"

Today I can answer each of those questions.

Yes. Yes. Yes. Yes. Yes. Yes. Yes. Yes. Yes. Yes. Ten times over, yes. My message to you is not "yes" and "no." As it pertains to God and his promises regarding our lives, it's always "yes." And through us—because we've seen the faithfulness of God's handiwork in our lives—we offer the blessed amen back to him and to anyone who is willing and ready to listen. We are the grace-filled, entrusted benediction of God's heart to his world. What he has done in us, through us, and most days, in spite of us, is a heaven-filled, from-his-heart "yes!"

What worthy, righteous trust he has placed into each one of us! We are kingdom storytellers, and by God's grace and because of his cross, we are the righteous witnesses to an everlasting truth. Every now and again, there comes a suffering to our lives, a cancer to our hearts, a poverty of soul that breaks us down and forces the issue of our faith. But even in those seasons, God is still the "yes." He didn't start being a "no" just because we're walking a tremendous road of struggle—no matter our doubts, no matter our fear, no matter our pains, no matter our tears.

God is "yes!" And we are the chosen amen of his heart.

What are you waiting for, friends? What coppers remain in your hand? Cast them into the treasury of God's heart, and see if he is not faithful to count them worthy for the kingdom. When you lay your all at the feet of our Rescuer, then you, precious ones, have given more than all the others. God will make your sacrifice count for all of eternity. He's the Promise Speaker and the Promise Keeper. He is our promised forever, from this moment forward.

Hold on to the promises of God. He who began a good work in you is faithful to bring it to completion. May the cancer that has sought to claim you instead become the means that God uses to rename you *Hope-filled Survivor!*

Thank you for joining me on this leg of my journey and for allowing me a few moments of your time. I count it a great joy and privilege to give to you this final gift of hope from my cancer season—Jesus Christ. He is the hope of my heart—my "next" and my forever. I pray he's yours as well.

God be with you, until we meet again. I look forward to seeing you on the road toward promise. Until then, take very good care of your hearts, and remember, the best is yet to be. Keep to it. Keep to Jesus. Thus, I pray:

You are more than I imagined, Lord, and far more than I asked for. You are faithful and true to your Word, and you are the hope of my heart, the certainty of my today and my tomorrow. I am grateful for and humbled by your trust. Father, take these words of my story—take my poverty and my pain—and multiply them to the glory and renown of your name. Today, even as I did forty days ago, I surrender my flesh into your hands. Mold me, make me, reshape me, and use me as you will for your kingdom gain. You are my "yes!" I am your amen. Blessed, sweet connection and communion—how could I ask for anything more? Amen. So be it.

Living Forward

- How is God using your costly surrender to further his kingdom purposes?

- When have you seen God's "yes" at work in your life? When have you been used by God as his amen to the world?

- What are some of the most important discoveries you have made since your journey with suffering began?

God Is Faithful

- Read 2 Corinthians 5:1–21. What are the responsibilities that God has entrusted to our care?

- How can you encourage others by applying the lessons learned from cancer's classroom?

Epilogue
Living Cancer Free

"The Spirit of the Lord is on me, because he has anointed me to preach good news to the poor. He has sent me to proclaim freedom for the prisoners and recovery of sight for the blind, to release the oppressed, to proclaim the year of the Lord's favor."
—Luke 4:18–19

I'M NOW SIX months out from my six months in. Over a year has passed since I first heard those words of initial diagnosis on a hot August afternoon in my oncologist's office. "Mrs. Olsen, you have breast cancer."

Today I hear other words, other phrases, to describe my condition. "Mrs. Olsen, you are cancer free."

Cancer free—the label I now wear. I'm not a huge fan of it. Long before I wore it, several of my cancer friends claimed it as personal identity. Proudly they displayed it, even more so proclaimed it, only later to be disappointed when their cancer returned. Perhaps this is the reason for my bristling suspicion of the label every time it is applied to my prognosis. Can I really, truly be cancer free? The skeptic in me says, "No." The realist in me says, "Get real." The martyr in me says, "Cancer is a better fit with my heart than freedom."

Setting aside my skepticism, realism, and martyrdom, there is still a struggle within me to accept my new medical status. A cancer-free diagnosis doesn't feel very freeing to me, not yet. Instead, it feels more like bondage, like being a prisoner whose sentence has been commuted but who is having a difficult time leaving the confines of her cell in order to embrace the walk of freedom. On paper, it doesn't make sense. Any logical, thinking person would be puzzled by the contradiction.

How can someone who has received the worst news of her life be conflicted when receiving the best news of her life? As a cancer patient, I don't imagine I'm alone in these feelings of inconsistency; perhaps, I'm just more willing to be honest about the struggle. And it's with this honest wrestling, this grappling with the truth, that a single point of light surfaces to guide me in my search for answers.

Perhaps living cancer free has less to do with a medical diagnosis and much more to do with a spiritual one. Healing of the flesh sometimes arrives sooner than healing of the soul. Active tumors may be removed from our bodies, but the hidden tumors that are fostered and nurtured in our hearts as a direct result of the physical tumors we've carried take a longer time to heal. That which cannot be seen and touched and manipulated by human hands is that which much be dealt with at a deeper level. For any of us to live free, whether from cancer or from another soul-eating "something," we need more than a medical determination from a doctor. Living cancer free requires a further determination from God—a soul-stirring, spiritual healing applied to our hearts because of the grace-filled understanding and release of the cross. We need the fullness of Christ's rescue as finalized at Calvary.

Jesus Christ spoke about that rescue the day he entered a synagogue in Nazareth and taught from Isaiah's prophetic renderings. It was a familiar teaching to the crowd—words about a sacred anointing yet to come, about preaching good news to the poor, proclaiming freedom for the captives, restoring sight for the blind, and releasing the oppressed. They were words of compelling promise that fastened the hearts of those who were listening to the voice of the one who spoke them. These words were not meant as a pep talk regarding an up-and-coming season but rather words spoken as a here-and-now fulfillment. "Today this scripture is fulfilled in your hearing" (Luke 4:21).

Today, freedom. Not tomorrow, next week, next month, next year. No, when Christ spoke about Isaiah's prophecy being fulfilled, he did so knowing that the time of fulfillment was at hand. Those who had eyes to see, ears to hear, and hearts to receive his words were those who were prepared to live cancer free. Free, perhaps, not from the torments of their flesh, but rather free from the torments of their souls—free to walk in faith and trust with the one God who would carefully and tenderly move them from a place of temporal poverty toward his wellspring of eternal promise.

He's done the same for us. Christ has come into our midst to present to us the good news of our freedom. His walk to the cross and his subsequent triumph over the grave give each one of us the opportunity for new life in the midst of an old, dying flesh. Even if we're carrying around in our bodies a physical tumor or two or none at all, we can

Epilogue

still walk our kingdom freedom. Jesus Christ is our ticket to getting there. The more we know him, reach out for him, fall into him, keep pace with him, the looser will be the chains that bind us to our infirmities.

It sounds simple, this cancer-free living, but I imagine it's been one of the hardest requirements of my faith journey. Getting beyond cancer's scars doesn't happen overnight. Laying claim to a stronger spirit takes times and requires intention—a deliberate willingness to do the soul work that leads to release. I'm not fully there, but on this day, six months out from my six months in, my scars no longer limit my forward progression. Instead, they serve as a living witness to the battle fought for my survivorship. I am a cancer survivor. More importantly, I am a soul survivor.

Thanks be to God for his marvelous surrender at Calvary and for the saving work of the cross! That which he came to do, he is doing in me. He is anointing me, freeing me, releasing me, sending me, and proclaiming over me the year of the Lord's favor. Today this scripture—this grace—has been fulfilled in my hearing and in your hearing as well. Freedom is calling you forward. Lend your ears to the truth, your scars to the healing, and your feet to the freedom walk of faith. Our best days are ahead of us. With Jesus Christ, our best days are always ahead of us. Thus, I pray:

Grant us courage, Lord, to live as a people free from the cancers that seek to destroy us. Calm our fears and insecurities with the truth of who we are because of what you surrendered. Humbly and willingly, we place the reins of control back into your hands and ask you to grow our trust in you for the road ahead. Move us beyond our scars to claim the stronger spirit that you desire to cultivate in each one of us. When the enemy fuels our aches with thoughts of wretched desolation, be quick to replace those lies with the truth of our holy consecration. You alone can loosen the chains that keep us from living cancer free. You are the freedom Giver, the freedom Leader, the freedom Sustainer. Give to us, lead us, and sustain us as we walk forward in grace. Amen.

Postscript

Beyond my scars.

It's been nearly three years since I wrote the closing prayer of this book, three years' worth of living beyond my scars. It's one thing to make bold proclamations about suffering; it's quite another thing to live them out most fully. Some days I still struggle with the scars that I see in the mirror and the ones that are less visible, hidden within my heart. Most days, I'm able to see beyond them, to celebrate them. But in all of my days, regardless of how I'm feeling, what I'm thinking, or what I'm seeing, there is one truth that has guided me, sustained me, fortified me, and saved me:

Jesus Christ—the Way, the Truth, and the Life.

Apart from Jesus, I can do nothing. Apart from him, my witness is nothing more than an infinitesimal chapter in World History that will soon be forgotten. But a life lived with Jesus, an entire existence shaped by his life, death, and resurrection? Well, those chapters are never-ending, chronicled in Kingdom History and forever remembered. And this is what it is to live most fully beyond the scars that have marked a journey with suffering. When you and I place our scars next to Jesus Christ and his scars—when we walk in the light even as he is in the light—our pain, our struggles, the pounds of flesh that have been extracted from our bodies, and the pounds of sorrow that have been added to our souls, are the makings of an extra-ordinary faith.

This is a life *beyond*. This is a life *better*. This is a life *blessed*. Therefore . . .

"Let us acknowledge the LORD; let us press on to acknowledge him. As surely as the sun rises, he will appear; he will come to us like the winter rains, like the spring rains that water the earth."

—Hosea 6:3

Keep close to Jesus, friends, and keep putting words to your stories. You are never closer to the kingdom of God than when you work alongside his Son and in the power of his Holy Spirit to share the witness of his good grace in your life.

Press on. Live forward. As surely as the sun rises, our Lord will appear!

elaine

If you would like to be in touch with me, please visit my website: PeaceForTheJourney.com. I would enjoy hearing your stories of grace.

Endnotes

1. "What Is Cancer?" American Cancer Society, http://www.cancer.org/Cancer/CancerBasics/what-is-cancer (accessed June 20, 2011).
2. Alicia Chole, *Anonymous* (Franklin, TN: Integrity Publishers, 2006), 15.
3. http://www.merriam-webster.com (accessed June 26, 2011).
4. Charles Spurgeon, *Morning and Evening* (NIV) (Peabody, MA: Hendrickson Publishers, 1995), 9.
5. Warren Baker and Gene Carpenter, *The Complete Word Study Dictionary Old Testament* (Chattanooga, TN: AMG Publishers, 2003), 1078.
6. http://studylight.org/desk/?l=en&query=Psalm+139%3A15-16&section=0&translation=nsn&oq=&sr=1 (accessed June 30, 2011).
7. http://www.merriam-webster.com (accessed July 8, 2011).
8. Spurgeon, *Morning and Evening*, 9.
9. William Killian, "Billy at 43," unpublished manuscript, 2010.

NyreePress

NyreePress Literary Group
"Publishing Life for Families"
www.nyreepress.com
www.buglovebooks.com
Twitter: @nyreepress

www.ingramcontent.com/pod-product-compliance
Lightning Source LLC
Chambersburg PA
CBHW080346300426
44110CB00019B/2525